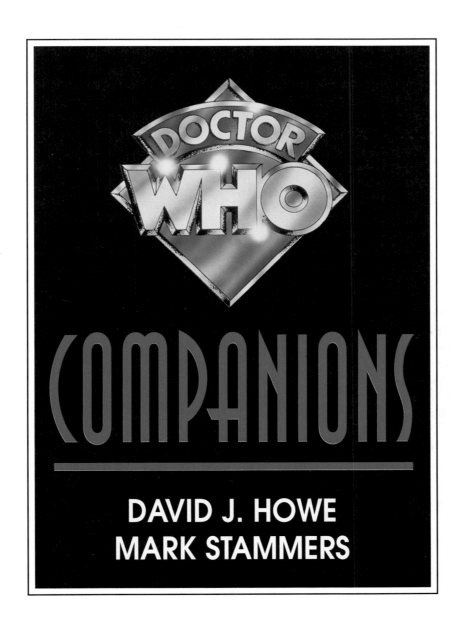

DOCTOR WHO

COMPANIONS

DAVID J. HOWE
MARK STAMMERS

DOCTOR WHO BOOKS

ACKNOWLEDGEMENTS

For help in preparing this book we are grateful to the following people and organisations:
Sophie Aldred, Keith Barnfather and Reeltime Pictures, Richard Bignell, Johnny Byrne, Stephen
Cambden, Paul Cornell, Michael Craze, Richard Hollis, Mat Irvine, Caroline John, Richard
Landen, Andy Lane, Tony Masero, Andrew Pixley, Elisabeth Sladen, Julian Vince, Stephen James
Walker, Richard Gregory and the folk from rec.arts.drwho.

For archive interview material we are primarily grateful to *Doctor Who Magazine* and Reeltime
Pictures' *Myth Makers* video series. Thanks are also due to many other magazines and
periodicals, including *TV Zone, Dream Watch Bulletin* and *In-Vision*, all of which have been a
useful source of information and quotes.

ILLUSTRATION/PHOTO CREDITS

Brian Aris, Associated Kent Newspapers, Richard Bignell, the Blinovitch Archive, *The Brighton
Evening Argus*, Steve Cook, Michael Craze, Raymond P. Cusick, Kevin Davies, *East Anglian Daily
Times*, Home Counties Newspapers, Hulton, Mat Irvine, Kentish Times Newspapers, Tony Masero,
John McLay, National Radiological Protection Board, Barry Newbery, Oxford and County
Newspapers, Robin Prichard, Reeltime Pictures, Scope Features, Neal Simpson, Lee Sullivan,
Syndication International, Andrew Thompson, *West Sussex County Times*.

Additional photographic research by Graeme Wood.

Every attempt has been made to contact the copyright holders of material featured within this
book. Any copyright holders of text or pictures inadvertently used without permission, please
contact Virgin Publishing.

First published in Great Britain in 1995 by
Doctor Who Books
An imprint of Virgin Publishing Ltd
332 Ladbroke Grove
London W10 5AH

This edition first published in 1996

Layout and typesetting by Mark Stammers Design, London, SM5 4LY

Printed and bound by BPC, Paulton Books

ISBN 0 86369 921 9

CONTENTS

INTRODUCTION

Much has been written about the Doctor and his many and varied travels through time and space, but surprisingly little has been revealed about the people he travels with. The role of the Doctor's companion was conceived partly to act as the eyes and ears of the television viewer, asking the questions that needed answering and providing a useful reference point for all who were trapped in the everyday environment of their sitting rooms.

This book is about those who have travelled with the Doctor. The people – mostly human, but occasionally alien – whose paths have crossed with that of the famous nomadic Time Lord and whose ordinary and mundane existence will not be the same again. Just as many people have memories of the different incarnations of the Doctor and the many adversaries he has faced, so too are his fellow travellers remembered. Perhaps you can recall Susan and her schoolteachers Ian and Barbara, or maybe Victoria, the prim and proper Victorian teenager. Perhaps Jamie, the irrepressible Scottish piper comes to mind, or maybe bubbly Jo Grant and serious Sarah Jane Smith. Do you recall Leela, the leather-clad savage with a heart of gold or K–9, the robot dog? Perhaps Tegan, the fiery Australian air-hostess rings a bell, or Melanie, the red-headed screamer from Pease Pottage. Finally there is Ace, the streetwise leather-jacketed teenager with a penchant for home-made explosives and action.

There are many character traits which observers and critics – mostly through the British media – have attributed to the Doctor's companions. Favourite among them is the comment that she (and it was always a she, the male companions escaped this label) was a screamer. Allied to this are the myths of tripping over and spraining an ankle, getting lost, asking the Doctor what is happening and running up and down lots of corridors. Some of these accusations are justified, and as *Doctor Who* progressed through the years, so the perceived weight of publicity of being the '*Doctor Who* girl' increased. The introduction and departure of the companions received as much press coverage as a change of Doctor, and although it was perhaps considered something of an accolade to appear in the programme at the time, several of the actresses have since raised accusations of their roles being sexist and, in some cases, actually harming their careers.

In this book we are exploring the background to the Doctor's companions. How and why did they start and end their journeys with the Time Lord? Who played the companions and how did they feel about it? We also look at some of the behind-the-scenes discussions and decisions that shaped this aspect of the series, and discover that casting a companion is rarely an easy decision to make.

David J. Howe
Mark Stammers
April 1995

WHY DOES THE DOCTOR NEED A COMPANION ANYWAY?

The first Doctor (William Hartnell) and his granddaughter Susan (Carole Ann Ford). The Sensorites.

The origins of the Doctor's need for companionship lie in the requirements of making a piece of dramatic and practical television as well as in his fictional past.

In the world of television production, there are many factors in play when considering what makes a good drama. First is to provide some sort of audience identification for the characters and the predicament that they find themselves in. It has long been an accepted part of the dramatic arts that the audience most closely identifies themselves with the character or characters who most resemble them. To this end, therefore, the producers of any drama series will seek to provide the basis for the widest scope of audience identification that they can.

In the case of *Doctor Who* the original production team knew that the Doctor was intentionally unknowable. He was the enigma at the heart of their mystery, and they did not want any of the viewing audience to identify with him. Therefore the other characters – the companions – had to provide that element of identification essential to a successful series.

Susan was introduced as a teenage girl partly in order to provide an identifiable reference point for the teenage audience, and partly to provide a focus for the series' intended educational aspect. Ian was the older 'handsome lead', a character type which was very much in vogue in the early sixties. Finally, Barbara was devised as an older 'attractive female', someone who could relate to Ian and the audience. The collective appeal of these three stereotypes and their relationships with each other was considered by the production team to maximise the potential audience.

Schoolteachers Ian Chesterton (William Russell) and Barbara Wright (Jacqueline Hill) watch from hiding as the mysterious figure of the first Doctor (William Hartnell) opens the door to a battered old police box, standing in a junkyard. 100,000 BC.

In fact, the technique of populating an ongoing television series with a 'family' of characters was commonplace at this time. *Doctor Who*'s family can simplistically be defined as Mum (Barbara), Dad (Ian), child (Susan) and grandfather (the Doctor). Other shows that followed this formulaic approach to casting were the three *Pathfinders* series that Sydney Wilson oversaw at ABC, *Z Cars*, and even *The Avengers* which initially featured John Steed and Doctor Keel and later introduced Carol Wilson and One-Ten in lieu of a single 'star name'. The concept of creating a show with a single lead started to gain prominence later in the sixties with series like *Adam Adamant Lives!* and

Maigret.

A rather obvious reason for having 'human beings' travelling with an 'alien' is to have someone to ask the questions that need to be answered. If the TARDIS was occupied solely by aliens, or by a single character, then either they wouldn't need to ask or comment about the environment or would end up talking to themselves to explain their thinking. By allowing the writers scope to answer questions, the plot and narrative can progress in a natural and effective manner.

There was one further reason why there were always two or more companions during the sixties. This was to do with a technical aspect of making a television drama. It was, at that time, very difficult to edit videotape. If numerous edits had to be made then the programme was generally telerecorded onto 35mm stock in the first instance, then edited to give a final 'cut' which was then transferred to video for transmission. Any editing of video that was carried out was 'in camera' as far as was practical and a single episode was recorded in as few continuous sequences as possible. For example, the pilot episode comprised just two sections, with the break occurring at the transition from the junkyard set to the TARDIS set. (In fact, there were actually four 'takes' to record the pilot episode as, following the sequences in the school and junkyard, there was a 'false start' to the interior TARDIS scenes, following which the TARDIS scenes were recorded twice.) This generally meant that the action had to be 'live' and that if, for

The third Doctor (Jon Pertwee) shows Jo Grant (Katy Manning) the view from the doorway of the TARDIS. Colony in Space.

The second Doctor (Patrick Troughton) explores a space beacon with his companions Jamie McCrimmon (Frazer Hines) and Zoe Heriot (Wendy Padbury). The Space Pirates.

Bonnie Langford (Mel) proposes drastic measures to remove the beard from Colin Baker (the sixth Doctor) during a photo call to introduce her character.

example, the scene cut from one set to another, then as the action on the first set neared its completion, the actors would take their places on the set for the second scene and recording would start from the end of the first scene as the cameras cut over.

What this meant in practice was that the same actor or actress could not appear in both scenes – it was physically impossible for them to get from the first set to the second set in time. If this restriction is considered in purely dramatic terms, then if the Doctor had no companions with him, the scenes would have to either feature him, or not. If there was only one companion, then every story would have to revolve around that companion getting separated from the Doctor so that scenes of the companion in danger could be interspersed with those featuring the Doctor. The only way to open the drama out and allow different combinations of actors on screen at any point, and to ensure that the story worked dramatically, was to have two or more companions.

As the sixties progressed, so technology advanced and by the end of the decade, it was far easier to edit videotape. This led to two developments. First, the more regular introduction in 1970 of out-of-order recording. This is where a story is recorded according to the requirements of action on a set-by-set basis rather than on a story-progression basis. This technique had become the normal way of recording *Doctor Who* by the end of the seventies.

The second development was the ability to reduce the number of companions to just one (or none in the case of *The Deadly Assassin*). During the seventies, the Doctor tended to travel with one humanoid companion (although he was teamed with both Sarah and Harry for the twelfth season) and since then, the number of travellers has been determined by requirements other than the purely practical.

When we first meet the Doctor, he is travelling – or, to be more accurate, has stopped travelling, as they have been on Earth for five months – with his granddaughter Susan. In the first story, *100,000 BC*, the Doctor comments that 'Susan and I are cut off from our own planet, without friends or protection.' This comment poses a number of questions, none of which is answered in *Doctor Who*'s history on television.

First: why are they cut off? In *The Sensorites*, the Doctor intimates that it is because he cannot control the TARDIS: 'This old ship of mine seems to be an aimless thing,' he comments. The later introduction of the Monk, another of his own race, suggests that perhaps the Doctor had left intentionally, and at the end of the second Doctor's era, in *The War Games*, it is revealed that the Doctor left his home planet (still unnamed at this point) in search of excitement rather than the tedium of observation which was the Time Lords' lot.

Later developments show that the Doctor is a traveller at heart as, given the opportunity, he will leave in his TARDIS at the end of whatever adventure he has been involved in. He even turned his back on the Presidency of Gallifrey in favour of continuing his journeys.

The second question posed at the start of the series is why Susan is travelling with the Doctor in the first place. We are simply presented with

Sophie Aldred (Ace) and Sylvester McCoy (the seventh Doctor) enjoy a break in the recording of Silver Nemesis.

Previous page: The fifth Doctor (Peter Davison) with his companions: Tegan Jovanka (Janet Fielding), Adric (Matthew Waterhouse) and Nyssa (Sarah Sutton).

The fourth Doctor (Tom Baker) searches for the segments of the Key to Time with the help of fellow Time Lord Romana (Mary Tamm). The Power of Kroll.

Tom (Mike Lucas), Jacob Kewper (David Blake Kelly) and the Squire (Paul Whitsun Jones) confront Polly (Anneke Wills) and the unconcious Ben (Michael Craze). The Smugglers.

her presence as a fact. The simple observation that the Doctor travels with others became one of the basic, essential tenets of the series.

Ian Chesterton and Barbara Wright, two of Susan's teachers from the local school, join the Doctor when, in order to prevent Susan from carrying out her threat to stay on Earth, he kidnaps them from the 20th century and whisks them away to what seems to be a random destination – in actuality stone-age Earth.

It is entirely possible that the Doctor's ultimate respect for and friendship with Ian and Barbara is what prompts him to offer a home to the others he meets on his journeys. There is possibly another reason, too: his granddaughter, Susan. The Doctor has a great deal of affection for her and when she falls in love with a freedom fighter in the 22nd century, he is forced to choose between his desire that she continue to travel with him and her needs as a fast–growing–up young woman. He chooses the latter and leaves her on Earth to follow her own destiny.

This leaves a yawning chasm in both the Doctor's heart and in the TARDIS and it is no surprise that, in his very next adventure, as soon as the Doctor realises that Vicki is an orphan with no future on the planet Dido, he offers her the opportunity to accompany him on his travels. He also sees a certain facial similarity between Vicki and Susan and his need for someone to fill the gap left by his granddaughter is great.

It seems at times that the Doctor is fated to share his adventures with others. No sooner has he arranged for Ian and Barbara to return to their own time using a Dalek time machine, than a battered and dazed astronaut, Steven Taylor, stumbles into the TARDIS. He is later discovered by the Doctor and Vicki, but too late to do anything but allow him to continue to travel with them.

The remainder of the Doctor's companions in the sixties seem to join him in somewhat contrived circumstances. Dodo enters the police box thinking it to be the genuine article; Ben and Polly enter on the pretext of returning Dodo's key to the Doctor; Jamie is invited; Victoria is orphaned when her father is killed on Skaro; and Zoe decides to stow away in order to travel with the Doctor.

In the seventies, the balance changes. Instead of two or three companions travelling with the Doctor, there tends to be just the one, and the reasons for the companion's presence have also changed. Doctor Elizabeth Shaw never actually travels in the TARDIS, although she does operate the controls on the console, and both she and Josephine Grant become associated with the Doctor through the United Nations Intelligence Taskforce, or UNIT, a paramilitary organisation whose British arm is led by Brigadier Lethbridge-Stewart, for whom the Doctor acts as scientific adviser during his exile to Earth.

After Jo comes Sarah Jane Smith, a journalist, who enters the TARDIS in search of a possible news story. Once she has savoured the delights of time travel – and has convinced herself that the Doctor is not the rogue she initially thought him to be – she decides to join him as a regular member of his crew. This decision is perhaps aided by the new, disarmingly friendly persona of the Doctor. Following his third regeneration, the Doctor became a far more social and personable traveller. Eccentric, yes, and prone to bouts of introspective philosophising, but generally someone who desired companionship. This leads to the Doctor gaining the trust and friendship of the savage Leela, who pushes her way into the TARDIS. It is with Leela that the Doctor sees another facet of his personality come to the fore: that of teacher. Leela is in many ways the perfect student. She is willing to learn and sees the Doctor as a powerful and influential shaman, someone from whom she can acquire knowledge. Alongside Leela there is K–9, who comes on board the TARDIS as a gift from its creator, Professor Marius.

The relationship with Leela eventually gives way to a far more equal partnering when the White Guardian sees fit to send another Time Lord to help the Doctor locate and retrieve the six segments of the Key to Time. Romana is in many ways the Doctor's equal and her superior attitude to many of the Doctor's traits and mannerisms ensures that their relationship remains stormy until Romana decides to regenerate into a form that the Doctor finds altogether more pleasing and with a personality that more closely matches his own.

Following Romana's departure, the TARDIS starts to get crowded again. Like Zoe, Adric stows away on the ship and is not discovered until the Doctor has left the boy's home world. Like Dodo, Australian air-stewardess Tegan mistakes the TARDIS for a real police box and gets herself hopelessly lost in its labyrinthine corridors. Nyssa, daughter of one of the Consuls of Traken, on the other hand, is orphaned when the Master steals the body of her father. She ends up travelling with the Doctor when the Watcher (himself an interim incarnation of the Doctor) brings her from Traken to Logopolis, thus saving her when the Master's interference results in the destruction of her home planet.

Then Adric is killed and Turlough, an agent of the Black Guardian and outcast from his own people, comes on board. Nyssa leaves to help others, Tegan becomes sickened with violence and walks out when the TARDIS arrives on 20th-century Earth, and Turlough leaves when he discovers that his own people have forgiven him. With Turlough's departure, the Doctor once again returns to just having one travelling companion at a time – perhaps the strain of overseeing so many people in such a short space of time was too much for his good-natured and optimistic fifth persona.

American botany student Peri teams up with the Doctor because she wants to travel and we don't know how or why Mel joins the bombastic sixth Doctor. Ace, the final companion of the seventh Doctor in his television adventures, joins because she is trapped on an alien planet with no future.

It is up to the individual viewer to make up his or her own mind as to which arrangement of Doctor/companion(s) was the most effective. Certainly no other fictional traveller has enjoyed as many or as diverse a selection of companions on his travels as the Doctor.

Frazer Hines (Jamie) and Deborah Watling (Victoria) attempt to keep warm on location in Wales for The Abominable Snowmen.

The third Doctor (Jon Pertwee) and Sarah Jane Smith disguise themselves in order to enter Irongron's castle. The Time Warrior.

WHO WERE THE COMPANIONS?

IN THE BEGINNING

SUSAN

The Doctor's grand-daughter, aged fifteen. She is a sharp intelligent girl, quick and perky. She makes mistakes, however, because of inexperience. Addicted to 20th Century contemporary slang and likes pop records – in fact, she admires the life teenagers enjoy in 1963. At the beginning of the story, she has persuaded her grandfather to stay in 1963 so that she can go to school and create at least one complete section of experience. Since she has been visiting all sorts of existences and places with her grandfather, Susan has a wide general knowledge and on some subjects can be brilliantly factual. On other matters, she is lamentably ignorant. She has something of a crush on Ian Chesterton.

Taken from format document prepared by David Whitaker. 12 July 1963.

The character of Susan had been evolved by BBC in-house writer C. E. (Bunny) Webber, *Doctor Who*'s story editor David Whitaker, the BBC's Head of Drama Sydney Newman and the head of the BBC's script department Donald Wilson during the many discussions developing *Doctor Who* that went on in early 1963. The first description of the character, taken from a format document produced in May 1963 by Donald Wilson, C. E. Webber and Sydney Newman, was as follows:

BRIDGET (BIDDY): A with-it girl of 15, reaching the end of her Secondary School career, eager for life, lower-than-middle class. Avoid dialect, use neutral accent laced with latest teenage slang.

Later that month the character was renamed Sue, then Suzanne, and finally, in July of that year, Susan.

The part had originally been cast by Rex Tucker during his brief tenure as *Doctor Who*'s producer in May and early June of 1963. Tucker later recalled that he had decided to cast 'an Australian girl' and the following actresses auditioned for the part on 25 June 1963: Maureen Crombie, Anna Palk, Waveney Lee, Heather Fleming, Camilla Hasse and Ann Casteldini. Also considered but not seen at the audition were Anneke Wills (who was later to play Polly in the series) and Christa Bergman.

Carole Ann Ford as Marguerite in Moonstrike – Five Hours To Kill, 1963.

Ping Cho (Zienia Merton) and Marco Polo (Mark Eden) confront the Doctor (William Hartnell) and his travelling companions: Susan (Carole Ann Ford), Barbara (Jacqueline Hill) and Ian (William Russell). Marco Polo.

THE TARDIS LOG

Name: Susan.

Origin: Gallifrey.

Likes: Pop music, behaving strangely, books on the French Revolution, hunky freedom fighters.

Dislikes: Being thought of as a child, scientific tests involving litmus paper, running up corridors, arranged marriages.

Joined the Doctor because: Unknown. Presumably he wanted the company. Or else he kidnapped her.

Left the Doctor because: He shut her out of the ship after she fell for a hunky freedom fighter called David. He grounded her, basically.

General Description: Airhead.

Scream Factor: ★★ Preferred to wail and moan a lot rather than to scream. Bit of a wimp really.

Previous page: Barbara and Susan at the magnificent palace of Kublai Khan. Marco Polo.

Opposite: Carole Ann Ford as the French Mistress, Mademoiselle Albertine in The Great St. Trinian's Train Robbery.

Below: Carole Ann Ford at the BSB Doctor Who *Weekend in 1990.*

Susan reveals some telepathic abilities when she encounters the Sensorites. The Sensorites.

A grown-up Susan is re-united with her grandfather in the death zone on Gallifrey. The Five Doctors.

Following Tucker's replacement by Verity Lambert in June 1963, she and Waris Hussein, the director of the first *Doctor Who* story, recast all the leads: one of the actresses originally considered by them for the part of Susan was Jackie Lane (who was later to play Dodo in the series). The part ultimately went to 23-year-old Carole Ann Ford.

She was chosen for the part by Waris Hussein, after he caught sight of her on a television monitor. 'There were viewing rooms at the BBC where you could watch what was going on in studio,' he explained, 'and I happened to see Carole acting in a show – what it was I don't remember. I went up to Verity's (Verity Lambert, *Doctor Who's* producer) office and brought her down to look at Carole on the monitors, and it was then we decided to ask her to come and audition for us.'

Carole Ann Ford has always recalled Susan as originally being a much tougher character, more akin to the Cathy Gale character in *The Avengers* and based in part on the Andromeda character from the BBC's 1961–2 series *A For Andromeda* and *The Andromeda Breakthrough*, but there is no evidence of this aspect of the character in any of the series outlines and scripts. Despite this, Carole asserted that she was not happy with the perceived change of direction. 'If I'd known I was going to be asked to do the lady I finished up doing for a year, I wouldn't have been quite so happy to do it,' she later commented.

The idea that Susan was the Doctor's granddaughter came from the writer of the first *Doctor Who* story, Anthony Coburn, and there was nothing within the format of the series to disprove this. The Doctor referred to her as 'my

'They saw I was a good screamer and offered me the part.'

Carole Ann Ford

granddaughter' and was always very protective and concerned for her. We discovered that Susan was more intelligent than human teenagers and yet she still enjoyed the simple pleasures of pop music. In fact, the only generally non-human characteristic that she was seen to possess was a telepathic ability which allowed her to communicate with the alien Sensorites without the use of the amplification devices that they themselves used. The Doctor also admitted to the talent, although this could have been a 'sixth sense' rather than any special power.

Susan was certainly very headstrong, refusing to bend to the rules of Aztec society when she found herself chosen by the so called 'Perfect Victim' as his bride – and, according to Aztec law, the Perfect Victim's wishes are never denied – and she was also brave, as witnessed by her lone flight back to the TARDIS to retrieve the radiation drugs in *The Daleks*. Although her schoolteachers knew her as 'Susan Foreman', this was probably not her real surname. It was the name written on the junkyard doors leading to number 76 Totter's Lane wherein the TARDIS was residing but there was otherwise nothing to link the name with either her or the Doctor, despite the fact that she was credited as 'Susan Foreman' on the closing credits of the show.

'It was a very weird set–up.'

William Russell

Ian (William Russell). Marco Polo.

Ian and Barbara investigate the junkyard that appears to be the home of their strange pupil Susan Foreman. 100,000 BC.

Joining Susan in the TARDIS were two of her schoolteachers from the local Coal Hill school, science teacher Ian Chesterton and history teacher Barbara Wright.

The male character had first been devised in March 1963 by C. E. Webber as a middle-aged man called Cliff, included in the line-up to appeal to older female viewers. This outline was then fleshed out and in May 1963, the following description was used:

27 or 28. Master at the same school (as Miss McGovern, later to be renamed Barbara). Might be classed as ancient by teenagers except that he is physically perfect, strong and courageous, a gorgeous dish. Oddly, when brains are required, he can even be brainy, in a diffident sort of way.

IAN CHESTERTON

27, red-brick university type, a teacher of applied science at Susan's school. A good physical specimen, a gymnast, dextrous with his hands and fortunate to possess the patience to deal with Doctor Who and his irrational moods. He occasionally clashes with the Doctor on decisions but for all the Doctor's superior scientific knowledge, is able to make intelligent enquiry and bring sound common sense to bear at moments of stress.

Taken from series format document. David Whitaker.

THE TARDIS LOG

Name: Ian Chesterton.
Occupation: Science teacher.
Origin: England, Earth, 1960s.
Likes: Knitted cardigans, dressing up, following Barbara, anything involving test tubes.
Dislikes: Schoolchildren who show him up in science lessons.
Joined the Doctor because: He was kidnapped after following Barbara into the TARDIS.
Left the Doctor because: He followed Barbara when she decided to return to Earth.
Companion most likely to: Pretend to be hip by singing and dancing to the Beatles, but end up looking like a sad cardigan-wearing science teacher.

Page 12: Barbara and Susan in the company of Jules Renan (Donald Morley). The Reign of Terror.

William Hartnell, William Russell and Carole Ann Ford rehearse a scene for The Aztecs.

The aspect of dexterity and physical prowess was then emphasised in Wilson, Webber and Newman's format document:

27, red-brick university type, the teacher of applied science at Sue's school. Physically perfect, a gymnast, dextrous with his hands.

Ultimately, Cliff was renamed Mr Chesterton by Anthony Coburn in a draft of his script for the first episode of *Doctor Who*.

Ian Chesterton was cast in July 1963 by Verity Lambert and Waris Hussein. They chose an actor named Russell Enoch who worked under the name William Russell. He had come to their attention through his starring role in the television series *The Adventures of Sir Lancelot* and was felt to have the necessary qualities to play the part of the staid and rather down-to-earth Ian Chesterton.

As played by William Russell, Ian was quite obviously there to provide a reference point for the viewing public. He was portrayed as a sceptic, initially at odds with the Doctor and his incredible claims of travel in the fourth dimension. Although he eventually came to trust the Doctor, his acceptance took longer than Barbara's, who seemed more open to the ideas and concepts posed by time travel.

'The first story seemed to us,' explained Russell, 'absolutely extraordinary, because we were sent back to the stone age. I'll always remember that because the actors had to do sort of Tarzan-type acting. We could hardly rehearse it we all laughed so much. Then, very quickly, we did the first Dalek story: that's when it really took off.'

As the series progressed, Ian settled more and more into the routine of time travel. He relaxed and started to enjoy himself, whether striding over the bleak and craggy surface of the planet Vortis, or lounging on a couch, eating grapes and drinking wine on the outskirts of ancient

THE TARDIS LOG

Name: Barbara Wright.

Occupation: History teacher.

Origin: England, Earth, 1960s.

Likes: Interfering in historical events, being followed by Ian Chesterton, hunky Thals, suave revolutionary resistance men.

Dislikes: Things that may damage her hair-do, being patronised, not being able to change history, insecticide.

Lookalikes: Tigellan High Priestess Lexa.

Joined the Doctor because: She was kidnapped by him, along with Ian Chesterton, when they forced their way into the TARDIS.

Left the Doctor because: She and Ian ran off together the first time they had the opportunity.

Companion Most Likely to: Read Mills & Boon romantic fiction.

Scream Factor: ★★ Only a few notable occasions, including her first meeting with a Dalek.

Opposite: Mistaken as the reincarnation of the high priest Yetaxa by the Aztecs, Barbara dons ceremonial robes. The Aztecs.

Right: A studio camera lines up for a shot, whilst Jacqueline Hill rehearses a scene in the corridors of the Dalek city. The Daleks.

Susan and Barbara enjoy the luxurious surroundings of the emperor's palace. Marco Polo.

Rome in the year AD64. He became involved in the adventures as well: battling the Aztec warrior Ixta to allow his friends to escape in *The Aztecs,* being sold into slavery in *The Romans* and even being knighted by King Richard in *The Crusade.*

Ian's character was considered to be very important by the production team: more so than that of Barbara. This was in keeping with the prominence given to male leads over female on television at that time.

The second schoolteacher, eventually named Barbara Wright, went through a considerable number of changes as Sydney Newman and his staff hammered out the concepts underlying the series. The embryonic character of Barbara was initially devised as a means of attracting older women to the series, as it was felt that the proposed younger female character would not catch their interest. In Webber's March 1963 character outline, the older female companion was simply described as 'The handsome well-dressed heroine, aged about 30'. By May of that year, Webber had updated his outline in view of the discussions which had been taking place between Sydney Newman and Rex Tucker. The older female character had become, by this time, a 24-year-old schoolteacher by the name of Lola McGovern.

On 25 June, along with the actresses auditioning for the part of Susan, Tucker also auditioned Phillida Law, Penelope Lee and Sally Holme for the part of Miss McGovern. As with the casting of Susan, Verity Lambert had her own ideas and she ultimately decided to

Jaqueline Hill in a publicity photograph for the first Doctor Who *story.*

Opposite: Vicki (Maureen O'Brien) and the hideous Koquillion (Ray Barrett), who is in reality Bennett in disguise. The Rescue.

Barbara and Vicki aid the supposedly disabled Bennett (Ray Barrett). He and Vicki were the only two survivors from their spaceship when it crashed on the planet Dido. The Rescue.

offer the part of Barbara Wright – as the character had been renamed during the writing of the first story – to Jacqueline Hill, a well-established actress who was married to one of Lambert's friends, television director Alvin Rakoff.

Barbara quickly became established as the mediator amongst the TARDIS's original crew. Even in the first episode of *100,000 BC*, when Ian flatly refused to believe the Doctor's seemingly ludicrous stories of time travel, she was willing at least to listen to the Doctor's explanations. In fact it was Barbara who was able to overcome the Doctor's initial mistrust of the two teachers, when she helped to solve the puzzle of the mysterious and frightening events that took place during the third story, *Inside the Spaceship*.

The history teacher's passion for her subject served her well during adventures in Medieval China, the Aztec civilisation of Mexico, Revolutionary France, Imperial Rome and Palestine at the time of the Crusades. Barbara and Ian relied on each other for support during their travels with the Doctor and there was an obvious and growing friendship between them even though there was never the slightest suggestion of a more intimate relationship developing.

It was in August 1964 that the decision was made not to renew Carole Ann Ford's contract. Ford was starting to look a lot older than Susan's supposed fifteen years and Verity Lambert wanted to introduce

a younger girl. Lambert decided that Susan would be written out in Terry Nation's second Dalek story. Ford's final regular appearance as Susan therefore came at the conclusion of *The Dalek Invasion of Earth*, which was recorded on 23 October 1964. It was some nineteen years later that Ford once again found herself playing the Doctor's granddaughter in *Doctor Who*'s twentieth anniversary story *The Five Doctors*. She had been asked back by the then producer John Nathan-Turner to reprise her role alongside Richard Hurndall playing the first Doctor, William Hartnell having died in 1975.

According to the plot of *The Five Doctors*, the Time Lord President, Borusa, was picking up the various incarnations of the Doctor, plus assorted companions, with a time-scoop device and depositing them in the 'death zone' on Gallifrey. Although there was a scene in the original scripts for the story where Susan was picked up by the time scoop while walking in an outdoor market, ultimately this was dropped and we did not see the location where Susan was picked up, but she was wearing modern clothes and

'All I ever
had to do
was look
frightened
and scream.'

Maureen O'Brien

was grown up. She was pleased to see her grandfather once more, even if they were immediately confronted by a rampaging Dalek.

'I nearly didn't do it you know,' Carole revealed. 'I turned it down when I first saw the script. I was horrified. They were writing Susan as if she were just one of the other companions, not his granddaughter at all.' According to Carole, she was told that the BBC did not want to draw attention to the fact that the Doctor had a granddaughter as that would imply that at some point he had to have had a sexual partner and that was taboo for *Doctor Who*.

Susan also re-appeared in the short *Doctor Who* skit *Dimensions in Time* made for charity on the programme's 30th anniversary in 1993. This appearance was little more than a cameo and was not explained in the context of the story.

The first Doctor and Vicki enjoy a riotous time in ancient Rome. The Romans.

A major consideration before casting a replacement for Susan was to ensure that the programme was actually going to run for long enough to warrant a new companion in the first place. Once agreement had been secured from the Chief of Programmes for BBC1, Donald Baverstock, Lambert cast actress Pamela Franklin to take over as the young female interest in the series. The new character was to be called Saida, later renamed Jenny, and introduced as one of the human resistance fighters on Earth in Nation's Dalek invasion story. Ultimately, this idea was dropped and the new companion was introduced in the following story, written by David Whitaker who was moving on from the post of story editor, to be replaced by Dennis Spooner.

Although it was known that the companion was to be a young girl, her name was less certain. David Whitaker's draft script for the story that introduced her was called *Doctor Who and Tanni* and the character's name went through several changes including Millie, Valerie and Lukki before being changed to Vicki during November 1964, at which point the script had been retitled *The Rescue*.

The part had actually been cast back in September, when two actresses, Maureen O'Brien and Denise Upson, were tested for it. It went to Maureen O'Brien after she performed a scene from *Member of the Wedding* as her test piece.

Maureen O'Brien had been working in the theatre, and the shock of moving to a television production was something she was not totally prepared for. 'I found it a completely alien environment,' she commented. 'The whole sort of middle-class, materialistic atmosphere of television was alien to me. I felt very scared and overwhelmed by the whole business.'

The character of Vicki was devised as being, at its most simplistic level, a replacement for Susan, but without the 'grandfather/granddaughter' relationship. This meant that the writers really had very little on which to base any development, which resulted in little being

Opposite: Vicki chooses to leave the Doctor and stay with her love Troilus (James Lynn) adopting the name of Cressida. The Myth Makers.

THE TARDIS LOG

Name: Vicki.

Origin: Earth, 2493.

Likes: Cute robots, hideous but friendly monsters, collecting rocks, being naive, Trojans.

Dislikes: Ammonia, pop music, having to grow up, spraining her ankle, being bored.

Joined the Doctor because: She was too hopeless to survive on her own.

Left the Doctor because: She fell in love with Troilus in ancient Troy.

Companion most likely to: End up being her own ancestor.

General Description: Futuristic airhead, reminiscent of Susan – strange that.

Scream Factor: ★★ Often let out squeals of excitement/fear/pleasure/disappointment. Bit of a squealer.

Vicki, the Doctor and the TARDIS's new passenger, astronaut Steven Taylor (Peter Purves). The Time Meddler.

Opposite: Steven and Vicki. The Time Meddler.

Maureen O'Brien poses for an early publicity photograph.

attempted. 'I thought of leaving very soon after I had joined,' she revealed. 'I found the role limiting to say the least. To look frightened and scream a lot is not very demanding to an actor.'

According to the plot of *The Rescue*, Vicki was a survivor of a colony ship that crashed on the planet Dido. According to a creature called Koquillion, all the other passengers and crew were killed on the ground by the native Didonians. Koquillion was the only friend that the survivors of the massacre – Vicki and a crippled man named Bennett – had. When the Doctor arrived, he revealed Koquillion to be Bennett, who had murdered the crew. When the murderer was himself killed, Vicki had nowhere else to go.

As Vicki had left Earth in the year 2493 and therefore was from 'the future', subsequent stories contained occasional throw-away lines referring to this; in *The Chase*, Vicki refers to 'Ticket to Ride' by the Beatles as being 'classical music'. Her character tended to be somewhat lively and inquisitive. Interested in most things, and keen to enjoy herself, she was also forthright with her opinions and was never afraid to let others know what she felt. In short, she was a pretty good replacement for Susan.

Both William Russell and Jacqueline Hill made their final appearances as Ian and Barbara in *The Chase*. William Russell had decided to leave in February 1965 and, after some contractual negotiations which could have resulted in Barbara continuing for a time, Jacqueline Hill also opted to leave in the following month. Therefore, as they had joined together, a decision was made for them to leave together. 'The only thing I remember about my final story was walking around London with Jackie (Hill),' explained William Russell when asked about this later. 'I always felt that the two characters were friendly but not in love or anything like that.'

Jacqueline Hill also remembered their departure from the series. 'We'd done two years of it, which was a bit of a strain and there wasn't a lot more we could do with it. Everything we wanted to do with the series had been accomplished and we felt – and I think Verity Lambert sneakingly agreed with us – that it was time for the series to try and see if it could do something new. As for the question of going together, well, it just seemed to come together at the right time for both of us. I think it had always been felt that Ian and Barbara, who had this slightly romantic side to their relationship, should go together much as they came, back to the London they left. They wrote us out well I thought at the time, and aside from the obvious sentiments, I can't remember having had any real regrets.'

'They'd decided at that point that the Doctor was absolutely the character and perhaps the companions should have less of a role.'

Peter Purves

THREE BECOMES TWO

Peter Purves at the BSB Doctor Who Weekend in 1990.

onsidering the strength of feeling on the production team that, aside from the Doctor, Ian was the strongest point of audience identification, it was not surprising that, when Ian and Barbara left, there was only one replacement character developed and cast as a handsome leading man of a similar age to Ian.

Terry Nation, who was at the time writing the third Dalek story, *The Chase*, was asked to include in his scripts a new male character who was to join the Doctor at the end of the story. By the start of April, this character's name had been amended from Bruck to Michael Taylor, introduced as a space pilot being held prisoner by the Mechanoids. The Mechanoids were a group of robots developed by mankind to prepare the planet Mechanus for colonisation prior to the human colonists' arrival. The problem was that the humans never arrived on Mechanus and when Steven Taylor's ship crash-landed there, the Mechanoids assumed that he was one of the colonising humans. Unfortunately, he didn't know the correct code-words and so they effectively kept him prisoner until the codes were issued.

The character was renamed Steven Taylor around the last week of May, just before recording started for the final episode of *The Chase*. Peter Purves, who was already playing a hillbilly American called Morton Dill in a sequence set on the Empire State Building in the same story, was felt to be right for the part. Verity Lambert approached him during the recording day on 14 May 1965 to ask if he would be interested in playing the part of Michael later in the story. He agreed

THE TARDIS LOG

Name: Steven Taylor.

Occupation: Astronaut.

Origin: Earth.

Likes: Toy pandas called Hi Fi, sarcasm, daft acronyms.

Dislikes: Singing in public, necktie parties, female clone warriors, catching colds, fat schoolboys.

Joined the Doctor because: He was being held captive by the Mechanoids, which can be quite painful, and escaped when the Doctor showed him how.

Left the Doctor because: The Elders and Savages on a distant world wanted someone impartial to lead them. Steven was volunteered and decided to stay.

Companion most likely to: Have a *Blue Peter* badge (apart from Ace).

General Description: A space astronaut, Steven Taylor never showed any aptitude for this occupation. Fond of blundering into danger on the pretext of looking after the girls.

Scream Factor: ★ Fancied himself far too much to be a screamer.

Steven and Dorothea (Dodo) Chaplet take a break from the deadly games of the Toymaker to admire each other's groovy clothes. The Celestial Toymaker.

and, on 21 May 1965, was contracted to appear in thirteen episodes .

According to Peter Purves, Dennis Spooner had thought through the character of Steven very carefully. 'I thought Steven looked smashing, a really good idea and we tried to find some sort of quirky thing for him to have, ending up with this Panda mascot that he carried about with him, though it could just as easily have been a pair of red spotted underpants!'

Peter felt that Steven's character was fine when it was being developed and written by Spooner, but unfortunately Spooner was on the point of leaving and handing over the story editing duties to Donald Tosh. It was in the first story of the third season, *Galaxy 4*, that Peter felt it started to go wrong. Part of the problem was that William Emms' script had been originally written with the characters of Ian and Barbara in mind, and their dialogue was effectively shared between Steven and Vicki: consequently, Steven got some of Barbara's lines and actions. Thereafter, Peter felt that the character seemed to become more of a cipher than a real personality, although he was allowed to stretch himself in several stories, most notably *The Celestial Toymaker* during which he and Dodo are teamed together to play deadly games in the hope of winning back the TARDIS, and *The Gunfighters*, which allowed for a touch of humour as Steven and Dodo take on the personae of travelling entertainers (pianist and singer).

When Verity Lambert moved on from the series, her replacement, John Wiles, together with Donald Tosh, decided that the time had come to change the female companion once more, and that Vicki should go. Actress Maureen O'Brien found out about this upon returning from a holiday, by which time Wiles and Tosh had agreed to write Vicki out in a story set in ancient Troy and to introduce a new companion, Katarina, in the same story.

Katarina, handmaiden to the prophetess Cassandra, was added to the last episode of Donald Cotton's *The Myth Makers* by Donald Tosh. She

'I knew I was going to be killed off before I joined.'

Adrienne Hill

Bret Vyon (Nicholas Courtney), The Doctor, Katarina (Adrienne Hill) and Steven examine the Dalek's tarranium core. *The Daleks' Master Plan*.

After leaving *Doctor Who*, *Peter Purves joined Valerie Singleton and John Noakes on* Blue Peter.

THE TARDIS LOG

Name: Katarina.

Origin: The ancient city of Troy, Earth, c. 1184 BC.

Likes: Pleasing the Gods (she thinks the Doctor is one).

Dislikes: The Greeks, wooden horses.

Joined the Doctor because: She was fleeing from the invading Greeks.

Left the Doctor because: She opened an airlock door during a struggle with an insane criminal called Kirksen, and was blown into space with him.

General Description: Your basic handmaiden from classical Greek mythology.

Scream Factor: ★★★ Not bad, although she wasn't around for long enough to tell for sure.

Above right: Sara Kingdom (played here by May Warden) is aged to death by the effects of the time destructor. The Daleks' Master Plan.

Opposite: Jean Marsh went on to great success in both acting and creating series such as Upstairs Downstairs.

Sara Kingdom (Jean Marsh), a Space Security agent from Earth. The Daleks' Master Plan.

joined the TARDIS crew by the simple expedient of helping Steven – wounded in a sword–fight with a Trojan warrior – into the ship at the story's conclusion. Wiles and Tosh very quickly realised that as Katarina was so innocent of life in general, it would be very difficult for any writer to give her anything to do. She was in awe of the Doctor and saw the TARDIS as his temple. She also had a firm belief in prophecy and spiritual matters but no elements of independence, an essential for good drama. Wiles and Tosh therefore decided almost as soon as they had written her into the series to write her out again and they instructed Terry Nation to kill her off in his forthcoming and fourth Dalek story, *The Daleks' Master Plan.* As a temporary replacement, they decided to widen the scope of one of Nation's characters, Sara Kingdom, and to use her as a 'companion figure' for the remainder of the twelve-part story, but to kill her off at the end as well.

By one of those strange television coincidences, Adrienne Hill, who was cast by director Douglas Camfield as Katarina, had previously auditioned for the part of Joanna in *The Crusade,* which eventually went to Jean Marsh. And Jean Marsh was cast as Sara Kingdom.

Adrienne Hill ended up filming her death scenes first. Katarina died in the fourth episode of *The Daleks' Master Plan* when she deliberately opened an airlock, sending her and the lunatic Kirksen, who was holding her hostage, spinning off into space. 'At my interview they asked if I had ever worked on a trampoline,' explained Adrienne. ' "Of course," I said. Then, when I arrived to do my day's filming, there was this large trampoline with cameras all round it and an instructor who proceeded to teach me and Doug Sheldon – who was the villain that was throttling me there – how to work on a trampoline. That was how it was done. It was all filmed from below with us moving from the trampoline. I have never been quite so sore in my life as I was the next morning.'

Appearing in only five episodes, Katarina was the shortest running of the Doctor's human companions.

Jean Marsh was hired to play icy Space Security Service agent Sara Kingdom by Douglas Camfield. She remembered appearing with the Daleks although it was the use to which her fellow cast members put them that was uppermost in her mind. 'No one was allowed to smoke in the

'The police box was a very badly built prop. It didn't show on screen, but it was very, very flimsy and I can recall turning a knob and watching it come off in my hand.'

Jean Marsh

THE TARDIS LOG

Name: Sara Kingdom.

Occupation: Officer in the Space Security Service.

Origin: Earth, 4000.

Likes: Uniforms, fratricide & travel.

Dislikes: Daleks, Mavic Chen and explaining to her mother what happened to her brother, being asked to take her clothes off.

Lookalikes: Princess Joanna, sister of King Richard the Lionheart; Morgaine, nemesis of King Arthur.

Joined the Doctor because: After killing her brother she is accidentally transported to the planet Mira with the Doctor and Steven.

Left the Doctor because: She was aged to death by the effects of the Time Destructor the Doctor used against the Daleks.

Companion most likely to: Buy gallon size tubs of skin cream to smooth away those wrinkles.

General description: Humourless, cat–suited, leather–booted, gun–toting nightmare.

Scream Factor: ★ Far too tough to be a good screamer.

Opposite: Dodo is caught by the Monoids, ouch! The Ark.

Dodo mistook the TARDIS for a real police box. The Massacre of St Bartholomews' Eve.

studio,' she recalled, 'and I am not a smoker, but many others were and they would ask the Dalek operators to get out of the machines so that they could climb inside and have a secret smoke inside the Dalek. Then smoke would curl out of the top of their casings and it would look ridiculous. It was just terribly funny.'

In the final episode of *The Daleks' Master Plan*, Sara suffered an horrific end as she was aged to death by the effects of the Time Destructor that the Doctor used to defeat the Daleks. Jean remembered the recording of her character's demise at Ealing studios. 'It was a good death by gradual ageing which was very effective. I remember the sweet old lady (May Warden) who played the final stage of my death, wearing my chic space uniform which I had worn throughout.'

After the departure of Katarina and Sara Kingdom in quick succession, Donald Tosh and John Wiles planned to introduce a new female companion called Anne Chaplet, played by Annette Robinson, in *The Massacre of St Bartholomew's Eve*, a story set in sixteenth-century France. The idea was eventually dropped partly owing to Tosh and Wiles' concern that the Doctor should not be seen to interfere too much in Earth's past history and partly for the same reasons that Katarina was dropped: the character lacked modern knowledge. They therefore opted to give the Doctor a more contemporary companion who was introduced in a short scene added to the end of the story by Donald Tosh, who had, in fact, rewritten all of John Lucarotti's scripts. In that scene, the TARDIS briefly materialises on Wimbledon Common and a young girl called Dorothea 'Dodo' Chaplet mistakes the ship for a real police box while trying to report an accident. The dialogue was meant to suggest that Dodo was in some way a descendant of Anne Chaplette although this was not absolutely clear in the final recorded version as William Hartnell accidentally omitted some of the explanation.

One nice touch which never made it to the screen was the planned inclusion of two passers-by as Dodo enters the TARDIS. As the ship dematerialised, they were to have turned and been revealed as Ian Chesterton and Barbara Wright. Although this scene was included in the story's filming schedule, it was not filmed for reasons unknown.

The actress who played Dodo, Jackie Lane, had originally been interviewed for a role in *Doctor Who* back in 1963. 'One day my agent phoned me up to ask if I would meet Verity Lambert for a six-part science-fiction story on television,' recalled Jackie when asked about this later. 'I have to say that science-fiction was not my favourite subject, but I went along anyway. In the course of the interview, they asked how I would feel about a year's contract and I said that I didn't want to be tied down for a year, which was perhaps the wrong thing to say as I then spent a year out of work. But at the same time I didn't think I was quite ready for it. I wasn't, however, actually offered the part.' In 1966, after a lean patch in her career, Jackie was offered the chance to play Dodo when John Wiles remembered her performance as a cockney character in a play that he had written, *Never Had It So Good*, at the Library

'It's difficult reacting to monsters because... well, they're not real!'

Jackie Lane

Dodo and Sergeant Rugg (Campbell Singer) play 'hunt the key'. The Celestial Toymaker.

Opposite: Polly (Anneke Wills) tends to the unconscious Ben Jackson (Michael Craze). The Smugglers.

THE TARDIS LOG

Name: Dorothea (Dodo) Chaplet.

Origin: London, 1960s.

Likes: Being a fashion victim, cruising accident blackspots, playing the piano, red hot nightspots, famous cowboys.

Dislikes: Being taken over by rogue computers, long dark corridors, telephone dating, games of any variety.

Joined the Doctor because: She mistook the TARDIS for a real police box when attempting to report an accident at her favourite blackspot.

Left the Doctor because: The Doctor packed her off to the country never to return.

Accent: Variable, occasionally theatrical cockney — Cor blimey guv — mostly standard BBC spoken English.

Scream factor: ★★★ Managed to fit a fair amount of ear-splitters into a short time with the Doctor.

Theatre in Manchester some years before. 'When the opportunity came up a second time, I thought I'd better not say "No".'

Wiles and Tosh had initially conceived the character of Dodo as a cockney, but were instructed by their superiors to drop the idea of her having a strong accent before the recording of *The Ark*. In fact, Jackie Lane was kept pretty much in the dark as to how her character should behave. 'Nobody talked to me about the character of Dodo at all,' she observed. 'The first I knew about it was when the first script was presented to me, so people talk about character analysis and what it meant to the series, but it didn't happen. It wasn't like that.'

As a contemporary girl, Dodo's dress sense tended towards trendy miniskirts and other typically sixties fashions, although the BBC hierarchy was extremely cautious about allowing the character to be too liberated. Steven and Dodo proved an adequate partnership although they suffered from a lack of character development and quickly became stereotypes.

'There was never a time when anyone talked to me about what this girl was really like. You just had a script and you had to bring something to it,' explained Jackie.

Innes Lloyd, who was replacing John Wiles as producer, and the incoming story editor Gerry Davis quickly realised that more changes were required to make the Doctor's companions more rounded characters. They felt that it was somewhat obvious that Jackie Lane was a good bit older than the teenage character she portrayed, and that Steven was far too solid and unimaginative to be interesting.

Peter Purves was informed by Innes Lloyd on 25 February 1966 that his services were no longer required. 'I was given three weeks' notice,' he explained when asked about it later on. ' "We're not renewing your contract," they told me. "What have I done?" I asked. "Oh, nothing, it's

Dodo races towards a date with destiny as she heads for a certain police box on Wimbledon Common. The Massacre of St Bartholomews' Eve.

'It was more than just another job. It was a great feeling of a very wonderful experience.'

Michael Craze

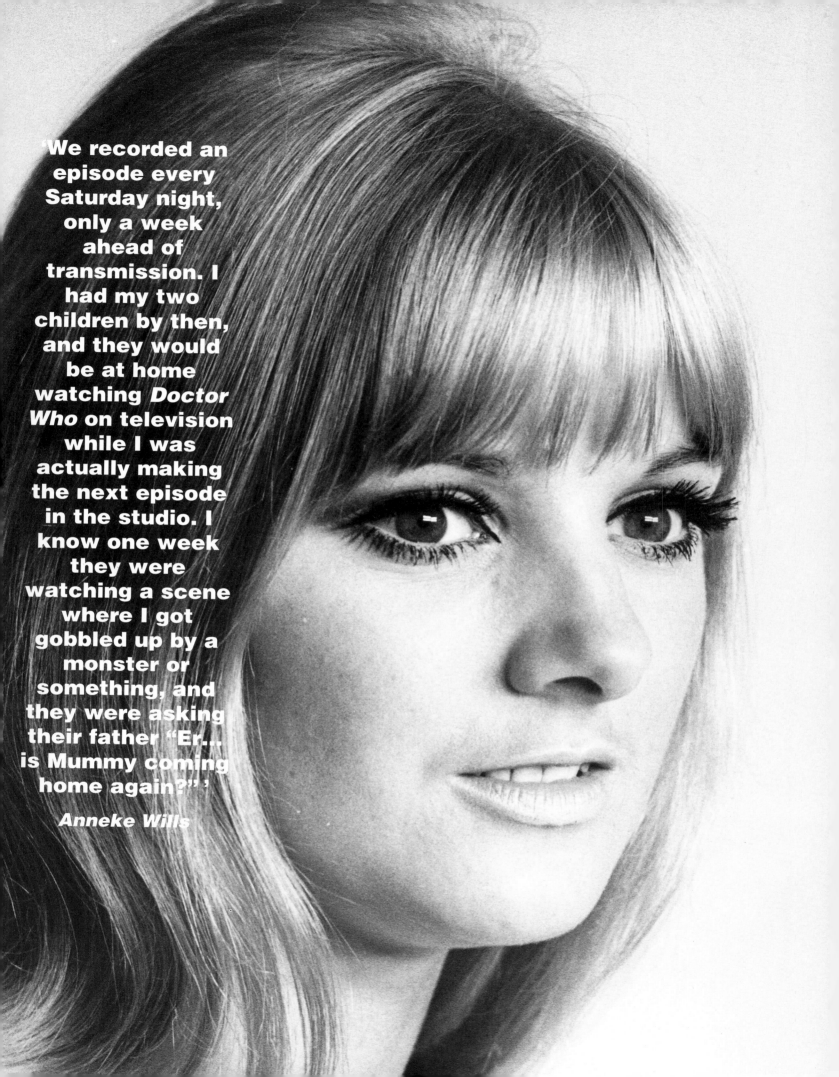

'We recorded an episode every Saturday night, only a week ahead of transmission. I had my two children by then, and they would be at home watching *Doctor Who* on television while I was actually making the next episode in the studio. I know one week they were watching a scene where I got gobbled up by a monster or something, and they were asking their father "Er... is Mummy coming home again?"'

Anneke Wills

just our policy." ' By Peter's own admission, however, he didn't have a great rapport with Lloyd and this may have contributed to the decision.

Jackie Lane was informed that her contract was also not being renewed in April of the same year. 'I was never consulted,' she stated. 'Actors weren't consulted about how they wanted to leave the series. There was a lot of violence in *Doctor Who*, and I think they decided on a gentler exit for Dodo.' After she had left the series, Innes Lloyd sent her a letter thanking her for her hard work and then adding, somewhat cryptically, 'I am sorry that because of the background etc., you were a victim of circumstance.' It is not known to what Lloyd was referring.

Steven and Dodo were ultimately written out in consecutive stories, Steven in *The Savages* and Dodo in *The War Machines*. Steven left to help unite the misguided Elders and the eponymous Savages on an unnamed planet after the Doctor helped them start the process of reconciliation and, after Dodo had been hypnotised by the power-crazed computer WOTAN, she was rather hurriedly sent to the country to recover after the Doctor released her from the machine's spell.

To replace Steven, the production team came up with a more streetwise character to be called Richard, or Rich for short. This was developed into the cockney Able Seaman Ben Jackson, on shore leave and looking for excitement.

Ben Jackson was intended to be a much more rough-and-ready character than Steven. Lloyd and Davis hoped that his naval background would provide the writers with an independent and resourceful character capable of being exploited when scripts required physical action scenes.

Actor Michael Craze was eventually cast as Ben. 'I was appearing in *No Hiding Place* when I got the *Doctor Who* part. I had watched *Doctor Who* before when I was in repertory in Harrogate. When I first went up I wasn't aware that the character was going to be continuing: I just thought it was going to be a one-off part in four episodes. Then they called us back and we had to do a piece for Innes Lloyd, and then I was called back again to do something for Michael Ferguson, who was directing that story. By this time I had realised that this was more than just the four episodes and that it was to be an ongoing

Able seaman Ben Jackson (Michael Craze).

Top left: Michael Craze and the rest of the Harrogate Repertory Company in 1965 relax between shows by watching Doctor Who *at their digs.*

Polly and Ben see inside the TARDIS for the first time. *The Smugglers.*

BEN JACKSON

24, Able Seaman (Radar), Cockney. Father, now dead, was wartime sailor and peacetime dock–crane driver. Mother married again to unsympathetic step–father. Ben trained at sea school from age of 15, having previously stowed away on cargo ship for adventure to get away from unhappy home. He enjoys the Navy and all it has to offer. Enjoys all sport, especially boxing and athletics – interested in all things mechanical and electrical and in true Navy fashion can turn his hand to most things, including basic cooking and sewing.

Temperament:
A realist, down to Earth, solid, capable and cautious. Inclines, on occasions, to be shy. He is slow to anger but somewhat thin skinned about his Cockney accent. (He thinks, mistakenly, that Polly looks down on him because of this.) He is also sensitive to Naval allusions made in fun – such as 'What ho, my Hearties' – 'Shiver me timbers' etc. He is intensely loyal and will risk anything for his two companions but won't take any nonsense from either.

Attitudes:
Wants to get back to his ship in Navy and resents Doctor Shanghai–ing him in the TARDIS – also resentful of Polly for getting him into TARDIS in the first place. Apart from this he respects Doctor but thinks him impractical – i.e. the way he cannot predict where the TARDIS is going in Time and Space. Rises to Polly's jokes about the Navy and the Doctor's cracks about his 'quaint accent'.

From undated, revised series Format Guide.

Top right: Polly and the newly regenerated Doctor (Patrick Troughton). The Power of the Daleks.

Right: Michael Craze. The War Machines

Opposite: Top: Michael Craze and Anneke Wills are reunited in a picture specially taken for the Radio Times Doctor Who *tenth anniversary special magazine in 1973.*
Bottom: Polly looks on as the Doctor consults his 500 year diary. The Power of the Daleks.

character.'

The story which introduced Ben was Ian Stuart Black's *The War Machines*, in which he was teamed with Dodo in the original storyline. Ultimately, Dodo was written out, and a new female character introduced.

The new character was called Polly Wright (although her surname was only revealed in a special audition piece written by Davis for the auditioning actresses to perform). Polly's character retained the elements of the fashion-conscious modern girl that had been part of Dodo's make up, but in a far less stereotyped form. Polly was obviously a product of the London fashion culture in which she had been living prior to her meeting with the Doctor.

Anneke Wills had been auditioned for the part of Polly by Innes Lloyd. She had been told that Polly was a contemporary swinging sixties character, which brought to the actress's mind the image of Honor Blackman as the leather-clad Cathy Gale in *The Avengers*. As this style of strong, independent woman was very much the vogue for heroines at that time, Wills decided to play against type by portraying Polly as, as Anneke later put it, a 'complete coward'.

In the series' format notes which were revised around April 1966, Ben and Polly were described in general detail:

They must have a <u>positive</u> and <u>active role to play in any story</u>. (From a production practicability point-of-view they should be written <u>to share quite a proportion of the stories with the Doctor</u> – this is so that the load isn't so great!)

They are not merely the <u>Doctor's acolytes but thinking human beings from this age, capable of individual thought and action</u>. They do not always agree with one another or with the Doctor – they are people with all the <u>strengths and frailties</u> – <u>inhibitions and forms of expression of which individuals are capable</u>. They are thrown together with the Doctor – Ben as a reluctant traveller, who feels that he has been Shanghaied into the TARDIS and <u>always trying to get back to the present day and the Navy</u>; Polly, also reluctant, but <u>enjoys the excitement of the unpredictable</u> travel although <u>when very frightened wishes herself back in the security of her friends and London</u>. NEITHER OF THEM MUST EVER LOSE A SENSE OF AWE AND AMAZEMENT AT THE FORM OF TRAVEL THEY FIND THEMSELVES UNDERTAKING. E.g. <u>They are real people transported into real situations in incredible adventures in Space</u>

THE TARDIS LOG

Name: Ben Jackson.

Rank: Able Seaman.

Origin: London, 1960s.

Likes: Polly, sailing, visiting exotic foreign ports, being pampered by beautiful women.

Dislikes: The idea of being AWOL from his ship, being thrown off ships.

Joined the Doctor because: He and Polly entered the TARDIS seconds before the Doctor operated the dematerialisation circuits.

Left the Doctor because: He ran off with Polly on the first opportunity they got.

Companion most likely to: get the girl.

THE TARDIS LOG

Name: Polly Wright.

Occupation: Secretary.

Origin: London, 1960s.

Likes: Fab clothes, going to happening clubs, dancing and being chatted up by dishy sailors.

Dislikes: Being controlled by pushy computers, any activity that might mess up her make-up or her stockings, giant crustaceans, injections, being mistaken for a boy.

Lookalikes: Chameleon Tours booking clerks, Michelle Leupii.

Joined the Doctor because: She followed Ben Jackson into the TARDIS seconds before it dematerialised.

Left the Doctor because: She ran off with Ben on the first opportunity they had to do so.

General description: Archetypal sixties dolly–bird.

Companion most likely to: move into fashion designing and win awards.

Scream factor: ★★★ Good enough at wailing to bring Ben running every time.

Opposite: Jamie and Victoria Waterfield (Deborah Watling) are pawns in the Daleks' schemes. The Evil of the Daleks.

and Time. They are ordinary people, with whom we sympathise, to whom extraordinary things happen.

As a general rule, Polly should find herself in dangerous situations from which either Ben or the Doctor, or both, rescue her. <u>She is our damsel in distress</u>.

Ben and Polly had little in common. Ben was a cockney seaman, while Polly enjoyed life as a society debutante, with a secretarial job. However, it was clear that the two characters were very much a couple, and they faced the dangers presented by the fact of their travelling with the Doctor together. Ben fell into the role of Polly's protector, and this facet was introduced at the outset as he physically protected Polly from the unwanted amorous intentions of a young man in the 'Inferno' nightclub ('the hottest place in town!').

Whereas Polly was very forward and extrovert, Ben was quite shy and retiring, occasionally a little ashamed of his more humble background and accent, which Polly occasionally made fun of. Their good natured jibes at each other, and Ben's adoption of the nickname 'Duchess' for Polly helped to make them into the more rounded characters that Lloyd and Davis had been looking for. It is also apparent that attitudes within the BBC were relaxing as Ben was allowed the accent that Dodo had been denied and Polly was allowed to wear the fashions of the period. 'Anneke and I were both of that period and we hit it off well,' recalled Michael Craze. 'She was a mad King's Road girl with all the latest fashions and all that. It was a great period, the sixties, despite what anyone says.'

The Doctor, Polly and Ben are captured by two Scottish Highlanders: Alexander (William Dysart) and Jamie (Frazer Hines). The Highlanders.

THE TROUGHTON YEARS

POLLY

21, Private Secretary to scientist. Father, country doctor in Devon, four brothers (one older – three younger). Happy and conventional middle-class background, she has never been tied to her mother's apron strings – they never know when to expect her home but when she arrives they are happy to see her. Has been, in turn, a travel courier, done a small amount of modelling (which she found irksome to her intelligence and feet) and when we meet her she is secretary to chief scientist on computer programme. She lives in a self–contained Gloucester Road flat.

She loves sports cars, watching motor racing, skiing, clothes, swimming – pet hates: pomposity, deb's delights, conforming and officials (police to ticket collectors). She is always ready to lose herself in a new pursuit – if it offers excitement.

Temperament:
Intelligent, imaginative, impulsive, inclined to act first, think later. Gets terribly frightened by unimportant things but is stoic about larger dangers. Sometimes forgetful and unpredictable. She is a sucker for lame ducks. Her warm–hearted sympathy for the under–dog, coupled with her impulsiveness, sometimes lands her and her companions in trouble. She is totally undomesticated – cannot sew, knit or cook.

Attitudes:
Has sisterly affection for Ben, though relies on him when they are in a tight spot. Teases him about the Navy. Resents Ben's domestic practicability. The Doctor represents a father figure but irritates her at times when he is being pompous or mysterious. She is also inclined to tease him as well.

From undated, revised series Format Guide.

Opposite: Jamie and the Doctor arrive on the windswept east coast of England. Fury from the Deep.

Right: Frazer Hines strips for action. The Abominable Snowmen.

Frazer Hines, Patrick Troughton and Deborah Watling take a coach to the location for the filming of The Abominable Snowmen.

The departure of William Hartnell as the Doctor and the introduction of a new face at the helm of the TARDIS as Patrick Troughton took over, heralded a small but significant shift in the way companions were perceived and used in *Doctor Who*. Michael Craze recalled that the atmosphere on the show changed at the same time. 'When Pat came in, he just changed the whole atmosphere altogether. It became so much easier to work. There was no atmosphere or anything, he was just free and easy, and once he had got over his initial nervousness and established the character, Pat was just a joy to work with.'

Although Ben and Polly were working well together, Innes Lloyd and Gerry Davis were still unhappy with the balance between Doctor and companions. They therefore took the step, for the first time since the departure of Ian and Barbara, of introducing a third companion.

James Robert McCrimmon, or Jamie, Scottish piper to the McCrimmon clan chief, started life as a minor character in a story written by Gerry Davis and Elwyn Jones – *The Highlanders* – set shortly after the battle of Culloden in 1746. Realising that the character showed potential, Davis and Lloyd quickly elevated him to the status of continuing companion. Frazer Hines was initially cast by the story's director, Hugh David, to play the young highlander. 'They said, "Would you like to do a *Doctor Who*?"'

'Mike Craze and Anneke Wills' characters' intelligence was different to Jamie's, they had seen cars and electric light bulbs and all that sort of thing.'

Frazer Hines

recalled Frazer, 'and I thought, "I've never done one, so yes, I'd love to." '

Hines had been contracted to appear in *The Highlanders* on 2 November 1966 and his contract allowed provision for three further options to be taken up on a further three four-part stories. The first location filming for *The Highlanders* took place from 14 November and on 21 November, an additional piece of location filming was undertaken, believed to have been a revised ending for the story in which Jamie travelled on with the Doctor. Jamie was included as a regular companion in the writers' notes issued on 28 November. Hines was contracted to appear in *The Underwater Menace* on 13 December, and filming for that story began the following day, just three days before the transmission of the first episode of *The Highlanders*.

As the character had been a reasonably late addition to the programme, subsequent stories were rewritten to incorporate Jamie. This was, on the whole, achieved by pairing him off with either Ben or Polly and splitting the written dialogue between them.

However, for *The Moonbase,* Jamie was simply rendered unconscious for most of the first three episodes – he hit his head while experiencing the reduced gravity on the Moon's surface.

Jamie was fiercely loyal to the Doctor, willing to sacrifice himself to protect his friend. In turn, the Doctor taught Jamie about the many scientific wonders which had originally appeared to the eighteenth-century boy to be the products of sorcery. This teacher/pupil relationship shaped the way future companions would be used within the series, especially during the second Doctor's era. So popular was Jamie with viewers that Frazer Hines

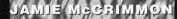

JAMIE McCRIMMON

He is a Piper, and the character must be that of a simple but engaging Scot. Although his smile disarms opposition, he is on occasions a man of action who will defend his friends or principles fearlessly. He is cheerful, open, manly, flexible – more flexible in fact than Ben and Polly. When either Ben or Polly are pulling his leg, he reacts with a grin. Because of his romantic appearance, he always wears the Kilt – his hair is longer and his shirt has a swashbuckling appearance: because of this and the attractive features of his character he must assume the part of the Young Hero in each story.

He must be constantly amazed and perplexed that he is wandering through Space and Time and is coming up against things, even common–place things, which he could never have dreamt of in his day. The large things – planes, computers, etc., rock him back on his heels – he finds it hard to comprehend them at all.

He brings many of the attributes of the Highlander of his period with him, being courageous, impetuous, superstitious and romantic. His impetuosity often provokes difficult situations for the time–travellers, but his direct approach will sometimes help solve problems as well as create them.

His superstitious background enables him to relate the forces of evil being fought by the Doctor to the witches, demons, goblins, etc., of his native land. Sometimes, in fact, this folklore gives him a deeper insight into the forces opposed to the travellers than the more scientific approach of the Doctor, Ben and Polly.

*BBC Character Outline.
28 November 1966.*

Top left: Jamie and Cully (Arthur Cox) on the planet Dulkis. The Dominators.

Opposite: Deborah Watling pictured in 1971.

Left: In 1995, Frazer Hines exercises his passion for horses at the stud farm he runs with his wife.

THE TARDIS LOG

Name: James (Jamie) Robert McCrimmon.

Occupation: Piper.

Origin: Scotland, 1746.

Likes: Haggis, wearing skirts, playing with his dirk, Polly, Victoria, Zoe.

Dislikes: Nasty cold draughts in awkward places, large furry beasties, jigsaws, being pampered by beautiful women.

Joined the Doctor because: He was invited to join the TARDIS crew by the Doctor.

Left the Doctor because: He was returned to his proper place in time and space by the Time Lords after they had captured the Doctor.

Frazer Hines and Deborah Watling encounter a Yeti for the Radio Times Doctor Who *tenth anniversary special magazine.*

Opposite and top right: Deborah Watling pictured in 1969.

The TARDIS brings Victoria and her fellow travellers to the Himalayas. The Abominable Snowmen.

remained with the programme right up to the end of Patrick Troughton's era.

With Jamie going down well with the viewers, Innes Lloyd began to think of replacing Ben and Polly, whom he felt had outlived their usefulness as characters. Michael Craze remembers his departure from the series as being just a matter of course when his contract came to an end: 'They came to us and said, "How do you feel about going?" and we said, "Well, we don't want to, really," because we were pretty financially secure where we were, but we didn't have much choice in the matter. My request was that I went out with a bang but they wouldn't have that. I would rather have been killed off or something, but as it was we went out like a pair of wimps. It was sad to leave, really, because we'd had a great time.'

Anneke Wills, however, recalls their departure slightly differently: 'Michael and I were offered contracts for another eighteen months, or whatever it was, but we both decided that if we didn't get out quickly we'd be so typecast that we'd never be able to work again. So although it was really hard to give up the security and the good money and everything else that went with it, as an actor you just have to keep moving on. We were sad to leave, though. I remember shooting our final scene, and it was really very emotional.'

In fact, according to the BBC's paperwork, both Michael Craze and Anneke Wills were contracted through until part two of *The Evil of the Daleks*. A decision was made to write them out earlier and so the characters were removed from the initial scripts for both *The Faceless Ones* and the following story, *The Evil of the Daleks*, although they still appeared in episodes one, two and six of the former story. Both artistes were paid in full for the episodes in which they did not appear.

As they had arrived together, it seemed natural for Ben and Polly to leave together. During the course of part one of *The Faceless Ones*, a story set on Earth in 1966 – the same year that Ben and Polly had started their travels with the Doctor – they dropped out of the action almost completely and did not reappear until the story's final episode to bid farewell to the Doctor and Jamie: they had decided to stay on Earth.

After deciding to drop Ben and Polly, producer Innes Lloyd and associate producer Peter Bryant had tried to persuade actress Pauline Collins to stay on as a regular companion after her appearance as Samantha Briggs, the concerned sister of a kidnapped holidaymaker, in *The Faceless Ones*. When Collins declined, David Whitaker was asked to revise his script for *The Evil of the Daleks* to take the character of Victoria Waterfield and turn her into a potential new companion.

Actress Deborah Watling was not the first choice for the role of the young Victorian orphan. Director of *The Evil of the Daleks* Derek Martinus auditioned a number of actresses for the role including two sisters, one of whom was Paula Challoner. A week after the Challoner

'When I came into *Doctor Who* it was lovely because Pat [Troughton] and Frazer [Hines] made me so welcome. It was brilliant, but on my first day in the studio I had terrible spots and you can see them. I came in on episode two and you see me trapped with this Dalek. I look at it now and think "look at that dreadful spot on your chin!" '

Deborah Watling

Deborah Watling returned to the role of Victoria in 1995, for the video drama Downtime.

Opposite: Zoe Heriot (Wendy Padbury) poses with a piece of equipment at a press call to introduce the character.

THE TARDIS LOG

Name: Victoria Waterfield.

Origin: England, 1866.

Likes: Screaming, finding out what Scotsmen wear under their kilts, fab and groovy sixties gear.

Dislikes: Being chased by big furry monsters.

Joined the Doctor because: Her father, Edward Waterfield, asks the Doctor to take care of Victoria as he lies dying at the end of *The Evil of the Daleks.*

Left the Doctor because: She stayed with the Harris family after her screams helped defeat the sea weed creature in *Fury from the Deep.* The Doctor may have arranged this to give his ears a rest!

Scream Factor: ★★★★★ The all time scream queen of the series.

sisters' second audition, six further actresses were auditioned. These were Celestine Randall, Elizabeth Knight, Gabrielle Drake, Tracy Rogers, Lanse Traverse and Denise Buckley. Buckley auditioned successfully and was booked to play the part, only to be replaced by Deborah Watling – who had auditioned unsuccessfully for the part of Polly a year earlier – on 13 April 1967, some seven days prior to the start of location filming for *The Evil of the Daleks*.

Deborah Watling had been spotted by Innes Lloyd on a *Radio Times* cover showing her as Alice in a 1965 BBC play about the life of Lewis Carroll. 'I've got that cover framed in my kitchen,' smiled Deborah. 'That year in *Doctor Who* taught me a lot about television technique. I learned a hell of a lot.'

Victoria was a typical Victorian-style heroine: innocent, modest and frightened of virtually anything that moved. She relied heavily on both the Doctor and Jamie to protect her from whatever monster lay around the next corner. Although her long nineteenth-century style dresses soon gave way to styles more suited to the sixties, Victoria's naiveté remained throughout her time in the TARDIS and her modest character was in direct contrast to her predecessor Polly.

After the death of her father at the hands (or rather suckers) of the Daleks, Victoria came to treat the Doctor as a surrogate father figure, and it was certainly true that the Doctor felt very close to the young orphan, often sharing his innermost thoughts with her. In *The Tomb of the Cybermen,* the Doctor tried to help Victoria cope with her grief over the death of her father by revealing that he kept the memories of his family alive in his mind. At the conclusion of Victoria's final story, *Fury from the Deep,* the young girl chose to settle down to a more stable life, remaining on Earth to be adopted by the Harris family. The Doctor was clearly saddened to see her leave, as was Jamie, who had become a protective older brother figure for Victoria. Later, in *The Two Doctors*, the

Molly (Jo Rowbottom) serves tea to Victoria and Ruth Maxtible (Briget Forsyth). The Evil of the Daleks.

Wendy Padbury poses for a publicity photo in her original costume.

Opposite: Zoe contemplates leaving the TARDIS. The Mind Robber.

Bottom right: The Doctor encounters phantom images of Jamie and Zoe in the Death Zone. The Five Doctors.

THE TARDIS LOG

Name: Zoe Heriot.

Occupation: Librarian.

Origin: Earth, early 21st Century.

Likes: Tight–fitting cat–suits, fashionable clothes, computers.

Dislikes: Not knowing the answer, not being right.

Joined the Doctor because: She stowed away on the TARDIS hoping for a little travel and adventure.

Left the Doctor because: The Time Lords returned her to her own time.

General Description: Diminutive, intelligent and pretty, Zoe's career prospects as an astrophysicist and astrometricist were not good. Unlike other companions, she didn't have aliens and other humans (except maybe Jamie) coveting her at every turn.

Scream Factor: ★★★★ After a good start she really let rip in the Land of Fiction, proving that her lungs are as capable as the best of the Doctor's companions.

Doctor commented that Victoria had intended to study graphology.

Victoria's screaming had become her trademark, and it was this attribute that was used to kill the parasitic seaweed creatures in *Fury from the Deep*. 'When I go to conventions now there's always some smart Alec in the audience saying, "Can you give us a scream please?" I have lost my voice so many times over that scream.' Deborah Watling took the decision to move on after only a year of playing Victoria, although in that period she had faced most of the best-known *Doctor Who* monsters – Daleks, Cybermen, Ice Warriors and Yeti – and she had even found herself acting alongside her father, Jack Watling, in the two Yeti stories, *The Abominable Snowmen* and *The Web of Fear*.

'I knew that I'd like to do about a year when I joined,' she explained. 'I also knew that they'd have liked me to do more than that, but I decided to go. I thought it was time, so I gave three months notice. You see, I'd learned a lot about television and I felt I had to get out and into theatre to learn something about that. They did try pretty hard to keep me on but no, I had to go. It was terribly sad, like the end of an era for me.'

Deborah Watling made a fleeting return to the role of Victoria in 1993, during recording for the short *Doctor Who* skit *Dimensions in Time*, where she accompanied Jon Pertwee's Doctor. Of more note was a 1995 direct-to-video drama production called *Downtime*, produced by Reeltime Pictures. Deborah Watling was once again playing Victoria and the story concerned the Great Intelligence's third attempt to gain a foothold on the Earth though mind-control. Jack Watling also starred as well as Nicholas Courtney, Elisabeth Sladen and John Leeson.

In keeping with the themes of change and development that were running through *Doctor Who* in the sixties, successive companions tended to be different from their predecessors, and when the time came to replace Victoria, the production team decided upon someone as far from a young Victorian as possible. This was Zoe, a computer-taught genius from the future.

Wendy Padbury was just one of a large number of girls, including Frazer Hines's then girlfriend Susan George, who were auditioned for the part of Zoe during January 1968. It was actually Peter Ling, the writer of the third transmitted story to feature the character, *The Mind Robber*, who came up with the character's name. In a letter to Ling written on 16 January, producer Derrick Sherwin commented that Ling's suggestion of 'Zoe' was the one that they would adopt for the character.

The character started off as being fairly atypical, as Wendy recalled, 'I liked her to start off with because I think

'It was the best job I've ever done, and certainly the happiest!'

Wendy Padbury

Frazer Hines and Wendy Padbury worked together once more in 1987, on the soap opera Emmerdale Farm.

Opposite: Brigadier Alastair Gordon Lethbridge-Stewart (Nicholas Courtney) directs his troops. The Invasion.

Wendy Padbury poses for a photograph in her costume from The Invasion.

Wendy Padbury as Zoe Heriot.

she was slightly different from a couple of the others who screamed a lot. She was an astrophysicist and was supposed to know what was what: she was fairly intelligent. Sadly, I think, with each consecutive story it was watered down, until I became a screamer again.'

Wendy later withdrew this comment after she had the opportunity to view some of her episodes again. She admitted that her memory had been wrong and that Zoe did not scream quite as much as she had remembered.

Wendy first met the rest of the *Doctor Who* cast when she attended the recording of the final episode of *Fury From The Deep.* 'Patrick Troughton has always been my favourite actor from when I was a little girl,' she recalled. 'It's very daunting when you're very young and you meet somebody you admire. But he made it very easy.'

Zoe was introduced in *The Wheel in Space,* written by David Whitaker. She was an astrophysicist and astrometricist with a pure mathematics degree with honours. Her role on the space wheel was as a librarian in charge of the parapsychology section, but her logical mind often led to the crew of the wheel using her as a second opinion. In fact, her reliance on logic and fact could also be her downfall, as the Doctor pointed out, 'Logic, my dear Zoe, merely enables one to be wrong with authority.'

As the character developed through her adventures with the Doctor and Jamie, so she matured. She was shown to be as intelligent as the Doctor in *The Krotons* and in *The Invasion* she destroyed a computer answering system with a logic problem and also helped UNIT to destroy the Cybermen's fleet in space by mentally calculating the correct trajectory for the only missile available to defend the planet. In general, Zoe came across as a strange mixture of the innocent and the intelligent. Someone who liked having fun but who was also perhaps a little too serious for her own good.

Zoe was written out of *Doctor Who* at the same time as Jamie, which also coincided with the end of the second Doctor's era. Although Padbury ultimately decided to leave with Hines and Troughton, she did initially consider staying on for the following season, only deciding to leave fairly late in the day. 'I really thought as Pat and Frazer were going it just couldn't be the same, so I thought it was an ideal time to leave,' recalled Wendy. 'It was sad, but when you've decided to leave a job, you're leaving it and hopefully going on to something new, so there was excitement too.'

According to the plot of *The War Games,* both Zoe and Jamie were returned to a point in space and time one moment before they left to join the Doctor, which meant that none of their adventures with him – aside from the one in which they first appeared – actually took place. It was this that alerted the Doctor during *The Five Doctors* to the fact that the images of Jamie and Zoe that he saw in the Dark Tower on Gallifrey were phantoms.

Jamie appeared in one final adventure with the Doctor. *The Two Doctors,* made around fifteen years after *The War Games,* involved the second Doctor and Jamie being sent on a mission by the Time Lords to stop a series of time experiments being funded by a scientist called Dastari. The Doctor's sixth incarnation also became involved.

A UNITED FRONT

The Brigadier meets his successor, Brigadier Winifred Bambera (Angela Bruce). *Battlefield.*

Opposite: Nicholas Courtney as the Brigadier.

THE TARDIS LOG

Name: Alistair Gordon Lethbridge-Stewart.

Rank: Initially Colonel, then Brigadier.

Origin: Earth, England, 1970s.

Likes: Doing things by the book, Doris, shooting aliens, having a pint.

Dislikes: Politicians, meeting himself aboard alien spaceships, dancing round a maypole.

Lookalikes: Sara Kingdom's dead brother, Bret Vyon.

First met the Doctor when: He was put in charge of a group of squaddies playing soldiers in the London Underground.

Companion most likely to: Be the maths teacher of your worst nightmare. 'Boy who failed algebra… five rounds rapid.'

General Description: Stiff upper lipped anglicised Scot, the very model of a modern brigadier.

F

ollowing the departure of the second Doctor along with Jamie and Zoe, *Doctor Who* was almost reinvented overnight. Gone were the sometimes whimsical adventures in space and time and in came solid science–based adventure on Earth. The third Doctor was played by Jon Pertwee and he had been exiled to the Earth by his own people, the Time Lords. This meant that the role, number and type of companions had to be rethought, and rather than persist with the 'one boy, one girl' approach which had typified the series over the last few years, a more radical concept was introduced.

The seeds of the military organisation called the United Nations Intelligence Taskforce – UNIT for short – were sown back in the era of the second Doctor, in a story which featured an invasion of the London Underground train system by horrific robot Yeti and a pulsing web-like organism. *The Web of Fear* took as part of its storyline the fact that London had been evacuated, and control of the Underground system was in the hands of the military. As the story developed, Colonel Lethbridge–Stewart was sent to take charge of the platoon of men holding a fortress close to Goodge Street Underground station, taking over from Colonel Pemberton.

Actors David Langton and Nicholas Selby were originally considered for the part – called simply Colonel Lethbridge in the early scripts – around mid-November 1967, but neither was interested. Finally, director Douglas Camfield decided to 'promote' actor Nicholas Courtney – whom he had previously cast as agent Bret Vyon in the William Hartnell story *The Daleks' Master Plan* – from the role of Captain Knight to the Colonel. Another actor was then brought in to play Knight. In fact, Courtney was not the first actor to be seen on screen as the Colonel, as Maurice Brooks stood in for Courtney quite literally: the first we see of the Colonel is a pair of feet which actually belonged to Brooks.

This would have been the first and last appearance of the Colonel, but a year later, the initial ideas for a Cyberman adventure set in contemporary London (initially called *The Return of the Cybermen*, renamed *The Invasion* for transmission) involved the return of both Professor Travers (played by Jack Watling) and

The Brigadier and the Doctor are transported to the Death Zone. *The Five Doctors.*

'I thought I was rotten in the part. It was a time when I thought, "Oh, I can't look at that, I'm terrible, I sound so posh."'

Caroline John

Colonel Lethbridge-Stewart, who had by now been promoted to Brigadier and was in charge of the newly formed UNIT group.

The BBC contacted the writers and creators of both these returning characters, Mervyn Haisman and Henry Lincoln, to seek permission to use them again which was gained on 7 May 1968. However, by the end of the month, more work had been done on the script and, as Peter Bryant noted in a memo dated 29 May, 'The character of Professor Travers is not one we can reasonably offer to Jack Watling.' In the event, another character was substituted called Professor Watkins and a decision was taken only to refer to Professor Travers without him actually appearing. In the case of the Brigadier, the production team realised that if Nicholas Courtney was not available for the required dates, this might cause problems. However, they decided that if this situation were to arise, then they would substitute another name and another actor for the character. As a mark of good will, John Henderson, the assistant head of copyright at the BBC, advised Bryant that, in either circumstance, they should pay Haisman and Lincoln for the use of the Brigadier. Luckily, Courtney was available, and so he reprised the role of Lethbridge-Stewart.

The idea of setting the seventh season's stories on Earth was one of the reasons behind Derrick Sherwin's creation of UNIT for *The Invasion.* Sherwin, who was at the time co-producing *Doctor Who* with Bryant, recalled that 'the idea was always to bring it down to Earth gently and then to stay there for a long period of time'. The approach of using a paramilitary organisation had previously been used in the *Quatermass* serials of the fifties and the idea of a scientific adviser was seen in a 1969 series called *Counterstrike*, where an alien was sent to Earth to help the humans repel other invading aliens, aided in the process by a female human doctor. Both of these series may have influenced Bryant and Sherwin's thinking with regard to the seventh season of *Doctor Who.*

It was during recording of *The Invasion* that Nicholas Courtney was asked by Peter Bryant if he would like to play the Brigadier as a regular character through the following season. He accepted at once, eventually signing his contract on 27 May 1969. This initial engagement was subsequently extended until the Brigadier ended up appearing in all but seven of the 24 third Doctor stories. He then appeared in two stories with Tom Baker (*Robot* and *Terror of the Zygons*), two with Peter Davison (*Mawdryn Undead* and *The Five Doctors* – which also featured the first Doctor) and one with Sylvester McCoy (*Battlefield*) in which the character was called out of

Nicholas Courtney (the Brigadier) and Caroline John (Elizabeth Shaw) on location for Spearhead from Space.

Left: The Brigadier had retired from UNIT and become a teacher by the time he met the fifth Doctor in Mawdryn Undead.

Nicholas Courtney reprised his role as the Brigadier in Downtime *in 1995.*

In an alternate universe, Benton is transformed into a Primord. *Inferno*.

Right: John Levene appeared as Benton in the video drama Wartime.

Opposite: Elizabeth Shaw (Caroline John) came from Cambridge to be UNIT's scientific advisor – a post usurped by the Doctor. Ambassadors of Death.

THE TARDIS LOG

Name: Benton.

Rank: Corporal, then Sergeant, then RSM.

Origin: Earth, England, 1970s.

Likes: Rugby, ballroom dancing (with his sister!), chatting up the ladies (they love a man in that UNIT uniform).

Dislikes: Being hit, fried, stabbed, shot, drowned or kidnapped by the latest alien monster attacking UNIT.

First met the Doctor when: The Brigadier got him to follow the Time Lord in a car.

Companion most likely to: Sell used cars.

General Description: Solid sort of chap, not all that bright but good at taking orders.

Favourite pose: standing with gun held limp, mouth open, muttering, 'I don't believe it!'

'I'm thrilled to have belonged.'
John Levene

retirement. He had to wait until the 30th-anniversary skit *Dimensions in Time* before he teamed up with the sixth Doctor in the form of Colin Baker. This gave Courtney the unique distinction of having played the same recurring character with all seven television incarnations of the Doctor.

Throughout this time, the Brigadier developed as a character, due mainly to Nicholas Courtney's input to the part. 'I was very firm about keeping him level–headed and sceptical at the same time,' said Nicholas. 'He knew he had a pretty fantastic job to do within the range of the Army, but it never threw him: he got on with it as the best soldiers do, calmly and efficiently.' Rather than try and keep the Brigadier as he was, successive production teams and writers showed the fictional character moving from Brigadier retiring to teach at a public school to being married and living in complete retirement in the country.

The Brigadier was a man who would never ask his troops to do something that he himself would not do: this resulted in him fighting personally the evil alien entities that seemed attracted by the Doctor's presence on Earth.

Like any good officer, the Brigadier surrounded himself with good and trustworthy men. Foremost among them was Sergeant Benton, played by actor John Levene.

Corporal Benton first appeared in *The Invasion* as one of the Brigadier's right-hand-men. Like Courtney, John Levene had been cast by Douglas Camfield from one of a small number of actors that the director liked to use. Camfield had previously cast Levene as one of the Yeti robots in *The Web of Fear*, and the part of Benton was the actor's first speaking role on *Doctor Who*.

In fact, the character received an unexpected boost at the end of *The Invasion* when, at a late stage, Benton took the place of Sergeant Walters in episode eight as UNIT's radio operator. A line was added to the dialogue to explain that Walters was operating 'the Geneva link'.

Benton did not appear again until the third story of the first Jon Pertwee season,

John Levene as Benton.

Liz and the Doctor (Jon Pertwee) have a little trouble with Bessie.

Caroline John in an early photo call for the part of Liz Shaw.

Opposite: Katy Manning as Jo Grant. The Mind of Evil.

THE TARDIS LOG

Name: Elizabeth Shaw.

Rank: Doctor.

Origin: Earth, England, 1970s.

Likes: Meteorites (she's an expert on them), short skirts.

Dislikes: Being seconded to work with UNIT. Being patronised by alien scientific advisors.

First met the Doctor when: He muscled in on her job as Scientific Adviser to UNIT, making her redundant.

Left the Doctor because: Well annoyed at having her cushy job snatched from her, she returned to Cambridge to sulk.

General Description: An eminent scientist with a penchant for short skirts which didn't really befit the serious nature of her profession.

Scream Factor: ★★ Rare, only under extreme circumstances.

The Ambassadors of Death. From this point onwards, he appeared in nearly every UNIT story, being promoted to Sergeant for *The Ambassadors of Death,* then to Warrant Officer in the second episode of Tom Baker's first adventure, *Robot* (although the end credits for that story still referred to him as 'Sergeant') and finally to RSM in *Terror of the Zygons.*

Benton's final appearance in *Doctor Who* came in the 1975 story *The Android Invasion* and the last we heard of him was in *Mawdryn Undead* when the Brigadier commented that he had left UNIT and was selling used cars.

Completing the complement for the seventh season was scientist Doctor Elizabeth Shaw, played by actress Caroline John.

After a succession of pretty young girls playing the Doctor's female companion, Bryant and Sherwin wanted something different. As the Doctor was to be based on Earth, working with a military organisation, they rationalised that the military group would need someone to bring a sound scientific basis to the varied alien threats they were there to investigate. Bryant and Sherwin therefore devised a scientific adviser to UNIT, someone who could act as an assistant to the Doctor, while being, theoretically at least, as intelligent as he was.

To play the Cambridge-based scientist, they cast actress Caroline John. 'I'd done quite a lot of stage work but I couldn't get into television,' she explained. 'So I sent a photo of myself in a bikini around to try and dispel the image of me as a classical actress. I got a lot of interviews, which was incredible, and got an interview with Derrick Sherwin and Peter Bryant, and they offered me this part. They told me that Jon Pertwee was playing the Doctor and they wanted to make the series more adult and they wanted a scientist sort of person. So I went out and got myself a sort of boffin pair of antique spectacles which I never wore, and that's how it started.'

The first story that Caroline appeared in, *Spearhead from Space,* was hit by industrial action at the BBC and all the studio recordings had to be hurriedly rescheduled to be filmed on location. 'First of all, we always did any outside filming,' she recalled. 'Before that we had a read through and I remember I was terribly nervous. With all the make-up and the costumes, it was exciting but I was a bag of nerves. Having done the first bits of outdoor filming, I was down at Ipswich and they told me that we were going to be filming in Evesham on the following day and I thought it was a joke: was this an April fool? But of course it wasn't, they had just forgotten to tell me about the strike. So I had to rush back to Ipswich, get all my stuff and get back up to Evesham in time.'

Caroline remembers the role as being quite snooty. 'I think she thought she was dabbling in something that was a little bit beneath her. I think she got on well with the Doctor because of his scientific knowledge which, of course, was way ahead of her own, whereas I think that she always felt UNIT was all soldiers and being silly boys.'

Following the setting up and casting of the seventh season, Bryant and Sherwin started to hand over to incoming producer Barry Letts and script editor Terrance Dicks, the latter of whom had actually started with

'As an actress, you're just doing a gig. For me, *Doctor Who* happened to be a terrific gig.'

Katy Manning

JO GRANT

Glamorous young female intelligence agent newly attached to UNIT, keen, professional, lots of charm. Works with the Doctor. Needs to be involved in the story in an active way, not just as a screaming heroine or passing the Doctor test tubes. Not a scientist, though with enough basic background to understand what's going on.

BBC Character Outline.

Mary Ashe (Helen Worth) and Jo.
Colony in Space.

Opposite: After leaving Doctor Who, *Katy Manning posed for a men's magazine in an attempt to dispel her* Doctor Who *image.*

Jo comes face to eye with the Federation representative from Alpha Centauri. The Curse of Peladon.

the programme at the end of 1968. As it happened, neither Letts nor Dicks were particularly happy with the scenario of the Doctor exiled to Earth, but had no option but to go with the stories that Sherwin and Bryant had already commissioned. For the following season, therefore, they planned to change things around slightly to open out the possibilities and relationships between the characters.

One of the first casualties was the character of Doctor Elizabeth Shaw. The problem as Letts and Dicks saw it was that she was an intelligent scientist, and was therefore at odds with the Doctor, not needing the explanations or protection that the Doctor had traditionally offered his assistants. They felt that this limited the scope of the character and so decided to write her out.

'That was at the end of *The Ambassadors of Death*,' smiled Caroline. 'I think Barry told me they were trying to find someone else. It was a two-edged thing because I hadn't known how to tell them that I was pregnant and I realised that it actually got me out of that dilemma and so it was sort of mutual. We parted on very amicable terms. However, they had booked me for the next season… I suppose they hadn't found anyone else and were leaving their options open.'

John returned briefly to *Doctor Who* as a phantom image of Liz Shaw seen by the Doctor in *The Five Doctors*, and also made a cameo appearance in the *Dimensions in Time* skit in 1993. The character of Doctor Shaw was, however, resurrected in 1994 for a direct-to-video drama called *The Zero Imperative*.

There was no 'farewell' scene for Doctor Shaw at the conclusion of the seventh season, and her absence the following season was explained as the character having returned to Cambridge. As a result, Doctor Liz Shaw was the only 'companion' never to have actually travelled in the TARDIS – although she did operate the controls of the main console as it was, for the latter part of the seventh season, removed from the TARDIS's main control room and relocated in the UNIT laboratories (or wherever else the Doctor wished it to be placed) so that the Doctor could work on getting it operational once more.

Barry Letts and Terrance Dicks were therefore looking for someone new, and they wanted a return to the more traditional companion of the sixties. A large number of highly attractive actresses were auditioned for the role of Jo Grant, including Anouska Hemple, Yutte Stensgaard and Shakira Baksh. After a day looking at this succession of tall, beautiful and perfect women, Letts and Dicks were undecided but then actress Katy Manning 'blundered' into the room they were using for the auditions – she had actually arrived late, got lost and gone to the wrong place. Letts and Dicks were taken with the bubbly, somewhat scatterbrained and

Katy Manning on location in Chislehurst Caves for The Mutants.

Opposite: Katy Manning pictured in 1974.

The Brigadier, Jo, Yates (Richard Franklin) and the Doctor discuss the Master's latest evil plans in The Time Monster.

Barry Letts directs new companion Katy Manning during location filming for Terror of the Autons. *This was the first time in front of the Doctor Who cameras for Manning.*

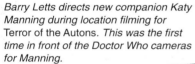

very short-sighted Katy Manning and, consequently she was offered the part. 'I used to love *Doctor Who*,' Manning revealed. 'I grew up with it, but I never thought I'd ever be in it.'

The original outline for the new character of Jo Grant was for someone perhaps more independent, but not as high-brow as Liz Shaw had been. With Katy Manning playing the part, the production team and writers naturally picked up on a lot of her own characteristics and this was one of the factors that allowed the character of Jo to develop. 'Doctor Who's other helpers seem all to have had something going for them,' Katy said in 1973, 'but Jo's really much more ordinary, though she gets better all the time. She's easily frightened, so it's fortunate that this Doctor Who is more capable than the others.'

Jo was a new recruit to UNIT and had pulled some strings with her influential uncle in order to secure a placement. She was assigned to the Brigadier who decided to put her with the Doctor. The Doctor was initially reluctant, claiming that he needed a fully trained scientist whereas all he really needed, as the Brigadier pointed out, was someone to hand him his test tubes and tell him how wonderful he was. Jo claimed to be a fully qualified agent, trained in cryptology and escapology and yet just about the first thing that happened to her was that she was hypnotised by the Master and made to open a bomb in UNIT's offices. After this, the Doctor mellowed towards her and even appeared to enjoy her company.

Jo was, in many ways, the perfect foil for

the third Doctor. She was, like many of the Doctor's companions, intelligent and resourceful, but her downfall lay in the fact that she was also slightly accident prone and tended to act first and think later – an endearing attribute which led her into danger more often than not. Katy Manning has said that she thoroughly enjoyed her time with the programme: 'I had a ball every day and there aren't many jobs that I can say have been such a consistent pleasure.'

Jo was definitely a product of the culture and fashion of the seventies. She had the same concerns and worries as those watching the series and was also independent enough to hold her own: whether on Earth or on alien planets.

The character of Captain Mike Yates was created as a possible love interest for Jo, although the writers never took this fledgling romance very far. There was also the fact that previously, there had been a succession of Captains serving under the Brigadier – Turner, Munro and Hawkins – and it was felt that it would be useful to standardise this into one role.

Yates's first appearance was in *Terror of the Autons,* where he reports from field patrol that two scientists are missing from the radio telescope used by the Master to contact the Nestenes once more. The Doctor also comments that Yates helped clear up the mess after the first Nestene invasion.

What lifted the character from being a rather run-of-the-mill officer-type was the production team's decision to have Yates ultimately turn traitor in *Invasion of the Dinosaurs,* a plot strand that had actually started in *The Green Death* at the close of the previous season. Yates had become involved in a misguided high-level conspiracy to return the Earth to a former 'golden age' through the use of a time-scoop device. Discovered and dishonoured, Yates resigned quietly from UNIT

The Doctor and Jo find themselves tied up while fighting the Daleks in Earth's future. Day of the Daleks.

Opposite: Katy Manning in predatory mood.

THE TARDIS LOG

Name: Josephine (Jo) Grant.

Occupation: UNIT operative.

Origin: Earth, England, 1970s.

Likes: Pulling strings, men, flared trousers, pointing and saying 'What's that, Doctor?'

Dislikes: Being thought of as being useless, Drashigs, daffodils, pollution.

Joined the Doctor because: She pulled some strings with her uncle and he got her assigned to UNIT.

Left the Doctor because: She pulled some strings with her uncle and got her future fiancé funding for a trip up the Amazon.

Companion most likely to: End up nude with a Dalek!

General Description: Blonde, enthusiastic, gets the wrong end of the stick.

Scream Factor: ★★★★ Likes nothing more than exercising her lungs.

MIKE YATES

The Brigadier's no. 2. A tough cheerful young soldier, very competent but a shade too easy-going and casual for the Brigadier's liking. Makes fun of Jo, in an affectionate way.

BBC Character Outline.

The Doctor boils off the explosive in the Master's bomb whilst Mike Yates and Jo look on. Terror of the Autons.

THE TARDIS LOG

Name: Mike Yates.

Rank: Captain.

Origin: Earth, England, 1970s.

Likes: Motorbikes, women, hot chocolate, shooting things.

Dislikes: Giant spiders, people who say 'om', dinosaurs.

First met the Doctor when: He was assigned to 'clear up' after the first Nestene invasion.

Left UNIT because: Went mad and joined a Buddhist temple where the appearance of giant spiders considerably improved his mental state.

Companion most likely to: Put a pair of underpants on his head and say 'wibble'.

General Description: Reliable Army man, likes the girls but Jo kept him at arm's length.

Twenty years after appearing in The Android Invasion, *Elisabeth Sladen finds herself back on familiar territory as Sarah Jane in* Downtime.

and began to attempt to put his life back together. Fate presented him with the chance to prove his honour when he discovered strange happenings at a Buddhist retreat where he had been staying, and he involved the Doctor in a terrifying battle against giant intelligent spiders in *Planet of the Spiders.*

Planet of the Spiders marked Yates's final regular appearance in the series, although the character appeared briefly as a phantom in *The Five Doctors.* Richard Franklin later wrote and produced a play called *Recall UNIT* or *The Great Tea Bag Mystery* for the Edinburgh Fringe Festival in 1984 which starred many of the UNIT characters, including Franklin reprising his role as Yates. Franklin has also written a book, unpublished as of 1995, called *The Killing Stone,* which concerns the future of Mike Yates after the events of *Planet of the Spiders.*

After three seasons playing Jo Grant, Katy Manning decided to move on and Letts and Dicks arranged for the character to be written out at the end of the tenth season. 'I left because I thought three years is about it,' Katy explained. 'I had to find out whether I could do anything else, and I think it's good for a thing like *Doctor Who* to change the girls every two or three years.' Jo had, over the course of her adventures with the Doctor, formed several romantic attachments: to Latep, one of the Thals on Spiridon; to King Peladon; and to Mike Yates. Therefore the most natural departure that she could make was to fall in love. This, not surprisingly, was what happened. She met and fell for prize-winning environmentalist Professor Clifford Jones in the story *The Green Death,* and, when he proposed to her and asked if she would travel with him up the Amazon, she agreed without hesitation. As an interesting aside, the actor playing Clifford Jones, Stuart Bevan, was going out with Katy Manning in real life at the time.

Jo's final scenes clearly revealed the Doctor being very moved by the loss of his companion and friend, and even Jo was sad to see their partnership come to a natural conclusion.

Following her time on *Doctor Who,* Katy Manning had become somewhat typecast as a dizzy scatterbrained bimbo, so in 1977, in an attempt to throw off this image she decided to pose naked with a Dalek for a series of pictures which appeared in *Girl Illustrated,* a men's magazine. 'I actually did them for *Playboy,*' she revealed later on, 'but as usual, somebody else gets hold of the pictures – the ones you don't use – and they go and print them in another magazine. I had actually done them for humour, thinking they were funny, but I suppose you had to be there.'

With the departure of Jo Grant, Barry Letts and Terrance Dicks had the job of introducing another companion for the Doctor. Terrance Dicks later recalled that they wanted a stronger character, less of a screamer; someone who was not the Doctor's assistant as such and who also regarded the Doctor with a high degree of suspicion at first. Thus a suitable character was created in the original outline of Robert Holmes' *The Time Warrior.* Dicks does not recall anyone other than Sarah Jane Smith being included as the companion, but there has been some confusion as to whether this was the original choice. Ultimately a script which included Sarah was completed and auditions were held.

'It really is sometimes quite embarrassing that people remember you with such affection, when you haven't done anything since. It's a wonderful bonus. I'm terribly pleased to have ever been part of it.'

Elisabeth Sladen

The UNIT team discuss the situation as marauding dinosaurs invade London. The Dinosaur Invasion.

The Doctor (Tom Baker) and Sarah attempt to escape the Kraals. The Android Invasion.

Opposite: The Doctor and Sarah at the old priory owned by Egyptologist Marcus Scarman. Pyramids of Mars.

The newly regenerated Doctor (Tom Baker) tries to convince Surgeon Lieutenant Harry Sullivan (Ian Marter) of his fitness. Robot.

Elisabeth Sladen had been recommended to the production team by the BBC's new head of serials Bill Slater on the strength of a performance she had given in *Z Cars*, and she proved to be the most suitable of the actresses auditioned.

'I was doing an advert the night before,' recalled Elisabeth, 'and it was very late when I got back. There was just a message for me to go and see Barry Letts for a part in *Doctor Who*. So I went along thinking I was auditioning for one story. I recognised Barry from his having been an actor and he seemed really pleased with me and asked if I would go to North Acton, which was where the rehearsal rooms were, and read this particular scene again with another actor, so that Barry could watch properly and have a chat with Jon. So I tootled along with Barry and Stephen Thorne, an actor with whom I have just recorded *The Ghosts of N-Space* for the radio. So I did the scene again and Barry seemed very pleased and he called Jon down and Jon came through the doors with two girls on each arm. I realise now that it was moral support because Jon's actually quite shy, but at the time it looked really grand. What I have been told about what then happened was that Jon chatted in front of me while Barry walked behind and gave the thumbs-up sign to Jon, then Barry went round in front of me, Jon came round behind and Jon gave the thumbs up.'

Sarah Jane Smith was far more liberated than Jo Grant. She was a journalist, used to getting her own way and prising stories out of others. One of the reasons that Letts and Dicks decided to make the character a journalist in the first place was because she could then legitimately ask questions and become involved in the plots without needing any other excuse. When we first met her in Robert Holmes' *The Time Warrior*, she had used the identity of her Aunt Lavinia – a notable virologist – to gain access to the Brigadier's 'safe house' of scientists. The Doctor realised immediately that she was not who she claimed to be, and agreed to keep quiet as long as she made the tea. As Sarah Jane was something of a feminist, this infuriated her and when the scientists started disappearing, she was determined to prove the Doctor's involvement. This determination led her to investigate the inside of the TARDIS and so she became an unwitting traveller in time.

Her inquisitive nature often got her into trouble as she insisted on going where she was not supposed to, and finding out about things that others wanted to keep quiet. As Elisabeth recalled: 'I asked Barry Letts at the start, "What do you want? What's she supposed to be like?" He said, "She jumps before she thinks – she's an instigator." They tagged the journalist thing on. So he left me alone, saying, "Just do what you think is right!", I thought they'd given up on me, actually. When you work on a play, you open your script and it says: the character is Sarah Jane Smith, she is so many years old, her father died the other day therefore she is seen in black, and so on. When I got my script for *Doctor Who* I opened it up and it just

SARAH JANE SMITH

Sarah Jane Smith was born in Liverpool's dockland in 1949.

Her father worked in a local newspaper office, but both he and his wife died while Sarah Jane was still young.

The orphaned girl travelled south to live with her aunt, the well-known scientist Lavinia Smith, author of *Teleological Response of the Virus*.

It was the royalties from this work, a major medical advance of the sixties, that enabled Lavinia to pay for Sarah Jane's education through school and university.

It was at university that Sarah Jane joined a newly founded magazine, *Metropolitan*. She wrote some acclaimed articles before becoming a freelance contributor with the right to choose her own assignments.

During this period she built up an impressive list of contacts. Among those she interviewed were Lady Collingford, the novelist Nigel Carter, and the Olympic Gold Medallist John Crichton.

But after a while Sarah Jane became bored with writing women's interest pieces. She wanted to write a strong scientifically based story.

While Lavinia was away on a lecture tour in America, an invitation arrived for her to visit a top-secret government research establishment. Sarah Jane impersonated her aunt and entered the complex. Here she met the physicist Joseph Rubeish and one Dr John Smith, scientific advisor to UNIT.

Dr Smith turned out to be a Time Lord, the Doctor in disguise, and after inadvertently stowing away on board the TARDIS, Sarah Jane spent three years travelling in Space and Time. (15.12.73–23.10.76)

Summoned to Gallifrey in 1976, the Doctor was forced to drop Sarah Jane back on Earth. They said goodbye on a bright autumn day somewhere in England, perhaps South Croydon.

From a format document for *K-9 And Company: A Girl's Best Friend*. John Nathan-Turner and Antony Root. 1 May 1981.

Top right: Harry (Ian Marter) and Sarah-Jane (Elisabeth Sladen).Terror of the Zygons.

said, "Enter Sarah Jane Smith," and I thought, "Oh, hello! Not much here!" In fact I was left very much on my own. What I didn't realise was that Barry wanted to see how much I had to give and obviously liked it. But I'm of the brigade of actors who think if no one gives them notes, they've given up on them! But we had a wonderful relationship and I had great respect for some of the writers and directors and indeed for Barry. Robert Holmes gave great ammunition to Sarah: in fact, I think that first story was the strongest they ever let Sarah be, they never dared let it happen after that.'

Elisabeth was not given much in the way of notes on which to base the character of Sarah, but she was able to draw a lot on her own character and experiences. 'I did draw on myself and my family. I remember watching my eight-year-old cousins a lot and I got some of what I thought were good body movements for Sarah, because I think there's an area of *Doctor Who* that can never be real. If you try to make the blood real, like *The Sweeney*, you've had it. It's got to be known to be tomato sauce and within that context, you have to be totally real. I used to think that you actually play a situation so it's as real as you can be and then you just notch it up fractionally, because I see the Doctor and his companion really as cartoon characters. You had to justify a lot of silly things that you did. You had to make them work the best you could. That was the format, you either had to be tied to the railway line or fall down a pothole every week, otherwise there was no story. So how do you do that week after week? You had to make it real in your mind, because if *you* don't believe it, no one watches you and if you don't enjoy it, no one watches. There was a great deal of enjoyment on *Who* otherwise it wouldn't have been so popular as it was.'

As Jon Pertwee was to stop playing the Doctor at the end of the eleventh season, Barry Letts and Terrance Dicks began working on ideas for the new Doctor and season twelve. Although no actor had yet been chosen for the role of the fourth Doctor, Letts's and Dicks's preliminary discussions had suggested that an older actor, perhaps less able to handle physical action scenes, might be picked. This in turn created the need for a new male companion capable of taking on the programme's action requirements which had been handled by the third Doctor in previous seasons.

Naval Surgeon Lieutenant Harry Sullivan was initially assigned to look after the newly regenerated Doctor by the Brigadier at the beginning of *Robot*, the first story to feature the fourth Doctor. He had been briefly

'I did and didn't like Harry. I responded instantly to his well-intentioned accident-proneness and his zeal for good and justice. But I did find his incompetence could become a bit of a drag.'

Ian Marter

THE TARDIS LOG

Name: Sarah Jane Smith.

Occupation: Journalist.

Origin: Earth, England, early 1980s.

Likes: Dogs, silly hats, Andy Pandy outfits.

Dislikes: Being patronised, anything alien and icky.

Joined the Doctor because: As a journalist she was good at sticking her nose where it didn't belong.

Left the Doctor because: The Doctor contrived an excuse to dump her when her moaning became too much to bear.

General Description: Professional journalist. Level headed, sensible, inquisitive.

Scream Factor: ★★★ Despite the professional appearance, Sarah is at heart a bit of a wimp.

Ian Marter pictured during the recording of his Reeltime Pictures Myth Makers video in 1986.

mentioned in *Planet of the Spiders*, the final story of the previous season, and had been called Doctor Sweetman in the original scripts for that story. Thus Harry was soon whisked off in the TARDIS along with Sarah Jane Smith.

Although Harry saw himself as the dashing hero, he was also very human and modest. This was combined with a brave nature that stood him in good stead. He was slightly clumsy with women, and had an old-fashioned attitude which infuriated the liberated Sarah, whom he tended to refer to as 'old girl' or 'old thing', much to her chagrin.

To play the part of Harry Barry Letts chose Ian Marter, who had originally auditioned for the part of Mike Yates at the beginning of season eight. Although that part eventually went to Richard Franklin, Letts remembered Ian and later cast him in the role of Andrews, a naval officer aboard the *SS Bernice* – a steam ship from 1926 Earth trapped in an alien miniscope – in the story *Carnival of Monsters*. The experience of playing Andrews was almost a dry run for the very similar character of Harry, and working on the programme gave Ian a foretaste of what working on *Doctor Who* as a series regular would be like. 'It was extremely hard work technically: we spent several days on a pensioned-off fleet auxiliary ship anchored on the River Medway, as I remember. There were a lot of special effects that inevitably caused problems but all the same, we had a lot of laughs with Jon Pertwee and Tenniel Evans.'

Once Tom Baker had been cast as the Doctor, it was clear that the actor would be able to handle all the physical action that the character of Harry had been brought in to take on. It was therefore inevitable that Harry Sullivan would not be long lived. Letts and Dicks had moved on, handing over the work of producing to Philip Hinchcliffe and script editing to Robert Holmes. The writers contracted to work on the series began to find Harry difficult to use and slowly the character fizzled out. After six adventures with the Doctor and Sarah, Harry elected to remain on Earth at the end of *Terror of the Zygons* and return to his UNIT duties, although the character would make a brief appearance three stories later in *The Android Invasion*.

Ian Marter remembered his quick departure from the series: 'I hadn't decided to go. Harry – the character (and that meant me too) – was dropped from the series because he had finally outlived his usefulness and was simply getting in the way. It was sad, but there you are. My own unfulfilled wish was that Harry could have been blown up while trying to save Sarah Jane, or something on those lines – a genuinely heroic exit instead of what I actually got.'

In 1986 Ian got the opportunity to give Harry the sort of send off he would have liked when he wrote an original novel, *Harry Sullivan's War*, for the expanding range of *Doctor Who* novels being published by W. H. Allen. Speaking six weeks before his death, Ian explained, 'I tried to make Harry a little bit more individualist and single-minded, not just reacting to things as they were happening. I originally thought of killing Harry off but the publishers wouldn't let me, and I don't think the BBC would have let me. I left it open ended at first but he's definitely alive at the end so he can obviously come back if he's required.'

Eventually Elisabeth Sladen also decided to stop playing Sarah. 'I'd worked for two producers. I knew I was Barry's choice and I knew Philip was really pleased to have me and I also knew there would come a time when Philip would want to put his own stamp on the programme. He kept calling us into the office to say, "Just look at these viewing figures," and I thought, this is so lovely, but it was also so important to me that I left when I was good.

Harry and the Doctor meet Vira (Wendy Williams) on The Ark in Space.

'I just did not want to be asked to leave, I wanted to go on a high, when I thought the time was right. You just go on a gut feeling. I think now maybe I could have stayed on just a bit longer. That would have been nice because it was so wonderful – I'm not using words indiscriminately, it really was – and I just wanted to go while that was there. It was probably the worst mistake I ever made, but the time was right. I also didn't want my last story to be about Sarah leaving because I don't think that the assistants can lead, I think they have to follow. I didn't want a story about being married off because I don't think it's about that, I wanted a good go at a story and then just decide, "OK, I'm sick of being shot at and hypnotised and whatever, I want to go, I've had it." I still think I'm right about that.'

Sarah's departure was very abrupt, as the Doctor unexpectedly received a call to return to Gallifrey. He claimed that he could not take Sarah with him and so arranged to drop her off on Earth. Prior to this, Sarah had been half-heartedly threatening to leave: to have her apparent wish granted so easily came as something of a shock to her.

As Sarah watched the TARDIS dematerialise after supposedly leaving her in her home town of Croydon, she suddenly realised that she wasn't in Hillview Road, Croydon at all. The final shot saw her striding off, whistling 'Daddy Wouldn't Buy Me A Bow-Wow' prompted by a labrador which had been sitting in the street as the TARDIS arrived.

Although Sarah had left the programme as a regular companion, Elisabeth Sladen reprised the role in the 20th-anniversary story *The Five Doctors*, in a number of episodes of *Doctor Who* on radio in the early nineties, in a one-off television programme, *K-9 and Company*, and in the video drama *Downtime*.

Sarah and Harry were the last of the UNIT family of companions.

THE TARDIS LOG

Name: Harry Sullivan.

Rank: Surgeon Lieutenant, Royal Navy.

Origin: Earth, England, early 1980s.

Likes: Playing the hero, calling Sarah 'old thing', sensible shoes.

Dislikes: Being dragged around the Universe by the Doctor.

Lookalikes: John Andrews, serving aboard the *SS Bernice* in 1926.

First met the Doctor when: He was assigned by the Brigadier to look after the newly regenerated Doctor. He was subsequently tied up by his patient and locked in a cupboard.

General Description: English to the core, Harry was one of the 'old school' who felt that most problems could be resolved over a good bout of fisticuffs. He was a gentleman too, treating Sarah as though she was made of porcelain, much to her chagrin.

ALIENS IN THE TARDIS

A nineteen-year-old Louise Jameson pictured in 1970.

THE TARDIS LOG

Name: Leela.

Origin: An unnamed planet in the far future.

Occupation: Warrior of the Sevateem.

Likes: Janis thorns, knives, hand-to-hand combat, killing people.

Dislikes: Not being allowed to kill people, wearing 'real' clothes.

Joined the Doctor because: She sneaked aboard the TARDIS before the Doctor left her planet.

Left the Doctor because: For an incomprehensible reason, she fell in love and decided to get married to a total drip of a Gallifreyan Guard Captain.

General Description: Leather-and-rag clad Amazonian female warrior.

Scream Factor: Leela would never scream. Her foes however, often do!

After the Doctor's solo appearance in *The Deadly Assassin*, Philip Hinchcliffe and Robert Holmes had considered leaving the decision of casting a new companion until the production break between seasons fourteen and fifteen. However, one idea under discussion was a character loosely based on Eliza Doolittle from George Bernard Shaw's play *Pygmalion*. The production team hoped that they might have been able to persuade Twiggy to take on the role, as this would tie into tentative casting ideas for the proposed *Doctor Who Meets Scratchman* film, although eventually both the character and the film failed to make it off the drawing board.

Hinchcliffe also considered offering the part to Emily Richard, an actress who had recently appeared in a BBC production of *Lorna Doone*, but she proved to be unavailable. In the meantime, Chris Boucher, the writer of the story following *The Deadly Assassin*, *The Face of Evil*, had been steadily working on his scripts. Leela had actually originated in a storyline called *The Mentor Conspiracy* submitted by Boucher before *The Day God Went Mad* (the original title for *The Face of Evil*) and subsequently rejected by Robert Holmes on 30 October 1975. Many of the character's eventual attributes were included in this outline.

Philip Hinchcliffe was impressed by Leela and mentioned to Boucher that they might use her as a continuing character incorporating some of the Eliza Doolittle elements of their earlier ideas. Boucher, unsure of the status of the character as he delivered the scripts, provided two endings to the story: one where Leela left with the Doctor, and one where she remained, so that the production team could decide whether they wanted the character to stay on or not.

'Leela was actually named after a Palestinian woman called Leila Khaled,' explained Boucher. 'She was one of the first hijackers. The character came out of the whole atmosphere of that time. The women's movement had begun to get under way: people in general and the media were beginning to see women in a different light. So I wrote this girl who was brave, bright, primitive, proud and curious and who, despite her basic naivete, didn't have the habit of deference. The production team liked this and said, "Yes, that's a good character." '

Leela was a savage warrior of the Sevateem. Her ancestors were from Earth, but after centuries of being marooned on an unnamed planet, half the crew – the survey team (Sevateem) – had reverted to barbarism while the other half – the technicians (Tesh) – became strange psychic guardians to a computer which had developed a split personality and which was calling itself Xoanon.

After auditioning over 25 actresses for the role, and arriving at a shortlist of five – Lydia Lisle, Susan Wooldridge, Louise Jameson, Janet Edis and Carol Drinkwater – Hinchcliffe finally offered the part to Louise Jameson. Once cast, Jameson had to undergo a number of tests of dark skin make-up before the production team decided to rely on the use of brown contact lenses – the name Leela was reported to mean

'I was literally getting scripts that had been written for Sarah Jane Smith. They changed the odd line for Leela, but there were still things like "Leela screams and runs and hides," and I said, "No, Leela doesn't." I had to fight long and hard on that one.'

Louise Jameson

Louise Jameson pictured in 1994.

Opposite: Leela (Louise Jameson), warrior of the Sevateem.

An early dark make-up test for Leela.

Leela and the Doctor investigate the scoop of a sandminer. The Robots of Death.

'dark eyed beauty' – and a skimpy leather costume to convey the image of a savage. The brief nature of the costume ensured a lot of newspaper coverage when the character was finally presented to the press.

Leela proved to be extremely popular, especially as the savage warrior broke the mould of screaming female companions, although for Louise Jameson it was a constant struggle to stop the script writers dragging the character backwards to become the standard screamer.

'In *Horror of Fang Rock* I was forever crossing out "Leela screams",' smiled Louise Jameson. 'At this point, I feel it wise to confess that I have a certain fondness for the story. Maybe it's because it's the one in which I asserted myself in the rehearsal room in a way that I hadn't before. I changed things for myself for the rest of the Leela era. I also got rid of those contact lenses that changed my blue eyes to brown.'

One person with whom Leela was not popular was the actor playing the Doctor, Tom Baker. Apart from a growing antipathy towards any companion sharing the Doctor's travels, Baker did not like the idea of Leela's extremely violent nature and requested that the production department modify the character to make her less vicious. Certainly in later stories, Leela would not kill people with the deadly Janis thorns that had become her earlier trademark.

An element of Leela's character which was not really developed was her latent telepathic ability. This was first referred to in *The Robots of Death* when she was able to sense both that the sandminer was about to experience problems and that Poul was not what he appeared to be. In *The Invisible Enemy* Leela felt that there was danger present when the TARDIS answered a distress call from Titan base. Aside from these cases, which could be ascribed to her

hunter's instincts, the concept was not employed any further.

By the end of the fifteenth season, Louise Jameson had made the decision to move on from the series. A combination of the short notice of her departure and the production team's hope that she would change her mind left Leela with an extremely unsatisfactory exit from the programme. She was married off to Commander Andred of the Chancellery Guard on Gallifrey at the end of *The Invasion of Time*.

'They were really trying hard to persuade me to stay. Graham Williams very flatteringly – even the day before we recorded the very last scene – said, "Come on, we could easily have you dive into the TARDIS. You don't have to go off and marry him. Please can you stay?" It was very sweet of him, but I'd already accepted the part of Portia down at Bristol... so I was already on my way.'

Leela adopts more conservative clothing for an adventure in Victorian London. The Talons of Weng Chiang.

Above: Designer Tony Harding's initial sketch for K-9.

K-9. A mobile computer in the shape of a dog which became the Doctor's faithful companion.

K-9 was created by the writers of *The Invisible Enemy*, Bob Baker and Dave Martin. K-9 was a mobile computer in the shape of a dog owned by Professor Marius who worked at the Centre for Alien Biomorphology – the Bi-Al foundation – located on asteroid K4067 in the asteroid belt between Jupiter and Mars. Marius, a specialist in extraterrestrial pathological endomorphisms, had arranged for K-9 to be constructed to replace his real dog which was left behind on Earth when he started his assignment at the Centre.

Graham Williams, who had taken over as *Doctor Who*'s producer from Philip Hinchcliffe, was quick to spot the potential appeal to younger viewers and was keen to have the metal canine continue in the series, not least because the prop had taken up a sizeable chunk of the season's budget and he was keen to see that initial expenditure put to practical use. As with Leela, the final decision to keep K-9 on was not made until late in the production of the story and two endings to *The Invisible Enemy* were recorded, one with K-9 staying behind, the other with him leaving with the Doctor.

The final form of the dog came from BBC Visual Effects designer Tony Harding, brought in to assist Ian Scoones who had initially conceptualised the prop. K-9's compact outer shell contained motors and lights that would make it roll along the floor, its ears move, its head bow, a gun nozzle extend from its nose, ticker-tape extrude from its mouth, its tail wag and

'It was the hottest, stickiest and most cramped job of my career.'

John Leeson

lights flash and blink on its back-mounted control panel. Unfortunately, its motors were erratic and noisy and the dog would often go haywire on the set as the cameras' electronic signals interfered with its radio-controlled systems. Despite its many problems, Williams decided to keep K-9 in the series.

Tom Baker was unenthusiastic about the metal mutt's arrival. He had been trying to convince the production team for some time that the Doctor had no need for any regular companions, even though this attitude had led to a somewhat strained working relationship with Louise Jameson.

Actor John Leeson was chosen by director Derrick Goodwin to provide the voice of K-9. Leeson became a popular member of the regular cast, owing particularly to his willingness to get down on his hands and knees and act out the part of the robot dog during rehearsals. Initially, his voice was modulated electronically to produce K-9's distinctive tones but Leeson, a talented voice artist in his own right, was soon able to dispense with the electronics and produce the voice himself.

As Williams had predicted, K-9 did indeed become incredibly popular with the general public. This was even more remarkable as K-9 was often absent from complete stories, mainly because the locations involved were unsuitable for its wheels. As a result of the interest generated in terms of publicity, Williams felt that he had been justified in introducing the dog and was also keen for some of the funds generated by the merchandise connected with it to find their way back into the programme's budget. As he commented in a memo to the Head of Serials, 'The programme has taken all the risks and by common market practice I understand that the greater the risk, the greater the return should be.' It is not known whether he was successful in his arguments.

John Leeson was replaced by David Brierley as K-9's voice for the last four stories of season seventeen (the dog did not speak in the first three, and the final story, *Shada*, was cancelled owing to industrial action at the BBC), but he returned for season eighteen, K-9's last season.

During K-9's time in the series, the prop underwent some repairs and rebuilding. The drive was changed from being rear-wheel to front-wheel and a specialist in radio control, Nigel Brackley, was brought in to operate the dog. Brackley continued to operate K-9 throughout its time on the series, aided by his assistant Stephen Cambden, and effects designer

K-9 poses with his operator, Nigel Brackley, and his voice, John Leeson, during rehearsals for The Stones of Blood.

Bottom left: K-9 was the only companion to earn a spin-off series, K-9 and Company.

K-9

Because of the weight penalties, Professor Marius of the Centre for Alien Biomorphology – the Bi–Al Foundation – was unable to bring his pet dog with him from Earth. Being somewhat sentimental, as well as eccentric, he built his data-analyser computer into the form of a dog and called her – him – it 'K-9'.

K-9 has many canine characteristics – he is loyal, brave and obedient. He also has several human traits – curiosity, stubbornness and a rather benevolent air of complete superiority towards other creatures, great and small. Although he claims to be a machine and therefore without emotion, he displays common canine attitudes; for example when a 'friend' approaches – his tail wags.

Professor Marius spent a great deal of time and effort to keep K-9 as companion-like as possible. The mechanical version of man's best friend has nuclear antennae for ears, computer printout for a tongue, a radio antenna for his tail and a blaster gun instead of teeth.

He is, as every 'K-9' should be, a loyal friend and formidable enemy. And sometimes quite infuriating.

BBC Character Outline.

K-9 made a brief appearance in the 1993 Doctor Who skit, Dimensions in Time.

Opposite: The Doctor and Romana. The Ribos Operation.

Bottom right: K-9's inner workings.

The Doctor, the Marshal (John Woodvine), Romana (Mary Tamm), Merak (Ian Saynor) and K-9 ponder The Armageddon Factor.

THE TARDIS LOG

Name: K-9 Mk I, II and III

Origin: Mk I's components originated on Earth, but he was built at the Bi-Al Foundation. Mk II was constructed in the TARDIS as was Mk III.

Likes: All kinds of data and information.

Dislikes: Water, steps and rough ground.

Soundalikes: The Nucleus of the Swarm, Swampie sympathiser Dugeen.

Joined the Doctor because: Mk I was given to the Doctor by Professor Marius. Mk II and III were built by the Doctor himself.

Left the Doctor because: Mk I chose to remain with Leela on Gallifrey where it could spend its days acquiring as much knowledge as it could handle. Mk II was damaged during the Doctor's attempts to leave E-space and remained there with Romana. Mk III was, bizarrely, sent to Sarah Jane Smith as a present.

General Description: A mobile box with a dog collar and gun. Fully TARDIS trained (apart from the occasional oil leak).

Mat Irvine took over the controls when Brackley and Cambden were unavailable. When the Doctor revealed his 'Mark 2' K-9 at the end of *The Invasion of Time* – the original robot having been left on Gallifrey with Leela – its colour changed from a grey-gold to a metallic charcoal. For the eighteenth season leading up to K-9's departure, the mechanics within the prop were completely rebuilt by Mat Irvine and one of his fellow designers, Charlie Lumm. Larger wheels were added along with two-wheel drive (rather than the original one-wheel drive which tended to make K-9 skid) and the radio control units were also upgraded from four- and six-channel AM Futba sets to six-channel FM MacGregor JR Series sets. The refit was completed in time and the 'new' K-9 made its debut in *State of Decay*.

With *Doctor Who*'s sixteenth season, Graham Williams decided to attempt something that had not been done before. He came up with the idea of linking all the stories together with a running theme and plot, and devised as the basis for the season a quest for the six segments of the Key to Time. At the start of the season's first story, *The Ribos Operation*, the Doctor was summoned by a being called the White Guardian and given the quest. To help him, he was also given an assistant, thus resolving the problem of how to introduce someone new following Louise Jameson's departure at the end of *The Invasion of Time* at the end of the previous season.

Williams had originally hoped to persuade Elisabeth Sladen to return as Sarah Jane Smith but Sladen eventually declined the offer. Williams therefore developed the idea of a companion who was the equal of the Doctor, and what better than another of his own race: a

Tom Baker and Mary Tamm rehearse a scene from The Stones of Blood.

Top right: A young Mary Tamm.

Opposite: Romanadvoratrelundar (Mary Tamm). The Ribos Operation.

Time Lord.

Romanadvoratrelundar, or Romana for short, was to be a recent graduate from the Time Lord academy on the Doctor's home planet of Gallifrey. She had gained a much higher level of achievement than the Doctor and revelled in showing her superior knowledge. However, her lack of practical experience outside the confines of the Capitol on Gallifrey often led her into trouble, which required the Doctor's help to extricate her. Romana believed that she had been sent by the president of Gallifrey to help the Doctor recover the six pieces of the Key that were spread throughout the universe.

The actress chosen by Williams and script editor Anthony Read after extensive interviews was Mary Tamm, who took on the part because of the different approach that was being taken to the standard *Doctor Who* companion. 'Romana was to be strong-minded, super-intelligent, sophisticated and attractive. Actually it was on that basis that my agent at the time persuaded me to try for the part. The character seemed so different, it seemed as though it was going to set a precedent for future assistants.'

Romana made her debut in the opening story of the sixteenth season and subsequently helped the Doctor to gather the pieces of the Key together successfully. She also faced off the White Guardian's opposing force, the Black Guardian, when he tried to trick the Doctor into handing over the completed Key at the season's conclusion. She in turn learned a great deal about life away from the stuffy confines of Gallifrey and her self-important 'know-it-all' stance mellowed a little.

However, despite an interesting on-screen relationship between the Doctor and Romana, the high promise of the early scripts soon faded and Mary Tamm felt that the character quickly began to slip back into the more standard role for a female companion. This contributed to Mary's decision to leave the series after only one season.

'I felt the role wasn't stretching me enough as an

'What I did enjoy about playing her was, for some of the time at least, she stood up to the Doctor and did something on her own accord.'

Mary Tamm

ROMANA

For the next season of 'DOCTOR WHO', the Doctor will have a new companion to assist in his quest for the Key to Time. She will be allocated to him by a Guardian of Time, initially against his own will and better judgement. She will, however, as the season progresses, prove her worth.

Romanadvoratrelundar, to give her full name, will not enjoy the full use of that name when she is with the Doctor. She will initially be furious at his insistence on the diminutive 'Romana' and even more furious at his sometimes mischievous further foreshortening to 'Romy'.

This will however provide part of the key to the developing relationship which will form between Romana and the Doctor.

Romana is an acolyte Time Lord (Time Lords still refuse to admit to an official title, Time Lady) who has been brought up to believe entirely in the Time Lords' principles of non–intervention and academic observation. She has been firmly placed in the Gallifreyan Groves of Academe and knows nothing of other worldly matters. She will, at first, be horrified at the Doctor's dismissal of the Codes of Practice which have been instilled into her education. As the season progresses, however, she will grow to appreciate the Doctor's sense of commitment and his breadth of vision. He, in turn, will be reminded of the youthful approach to problems and situations which, on occasion, will slip by his more sophisticated approach. He will be sometimes surprised, and even annoyed at her knowledge of later techniques than were available to him during <u>his</u> undergraduate years.

Physically, Romana is a beautiful girl with an earthly appearance of about twenty years – she may, at the end of the season, be due for her first regeneration, which would make her in Gallifreyan terms, a mere hundred and forty year old slip of a girl. She possesses the virtues of youthful impetuousness, courage, agility – and an agility not only of body, but also of mind. She can therefore be expected to overcome the hidebound nature of her upbringing and slowly adapt to new patterns of thought and behaviour. Hence her selection by the Guardian. She will, for example, eventually see the sense in the Doctor's rather biting criticisms of her wearing the full length dress as being somewhat impractical and will, to his astonishment, hack it off above the knee to give herself more freedom of movement.

The Doctor will, as always, mistrust anyone's judgement but his own. He may, therefore, not give Romana the full facts of any situation, but try, even, to mislead her. As he grows to know and respect her through her own powers of logic and deduction he will combine his own formidable powers with her latent talents.

Whilst her vulnerability will be born of inexperience, that same inexperience provides her with a freedom of temperament which, when unleashed, makes her actions as unpredictable and as mischievous as the Doctor's. She is, in short, the perfect foil to the Doctor in any situation throughout Time and Space.

**BBC Character Outline. Graham Williams.
10 October 1977.**

*Right: Romana finds the fourth segment
of the Key. The Androids of Tara.*

*Opposite: The Doctor and Romana
(Lalla Ward) in Professor Chronotis's
study. Shada. Insets: Before settling on
her final post-regeneration appearance,
Romana tried these three other bodies.
Destiny of the Daleks.*

*The Doctor and Romana try to recover the second part of the Key to Time from
The Pirate Planet.*

actress and therefore I was not prepared to tag along behind Tom Baker for another nine months just feeding him lines. Both my agent and I kept telling Graham Williams that I would not be staying but I don't think he ever believed me until it was too late. So there was no "Goodbye Doctor" scene.'

The difficulty of explaining away the departure of one companion and the arrival of a new one between seasons was ultimately solved by Romana's Time-Lord biology. As the Doctor had regenerated before, so could Romana. This idea had, in fact, been mooted in the character outline for Romana prepared by Graham Williams at the start of the sixteenth season. Williams and new script editor Douglas Adams briefly toyed with the idea of having the character played by a different actress in each story, but in the end the role of Romana's second incarnation was given to actress Lalla Ward.

Lalla had been cast by director Michael Hayes as Princess Astra in the final story of season sixteen, *The Armageddon Factor*. It wasn't until that story was completed that she was asked to come and play Romana.

'There comes a point as an actor when it's a very beguiling thought to be in a series, it's not even just the money, it's the knowing what you're doing next and knowing really for quite a long time. I fell for that and I had a very happy time doing it.'

Lalla Ward

A very young Lalla Ward in 1967.

Above right: Lalla Ward pictured in 1994.

Right: Lalla Ward and Tom Baker were married in December 1980. The marriage only lasted 16 months.

Opposite: The second incarnation of Romana (Lalla Ward). Full Circle.

'I think Tom suggested me,' she explained. 'We'd got on very well and there's never been anything in *Doctor Who* which says you can't play Princess Astra before you play a companion. Graham rang me up and asked if I would ike to come out to lunch and I said, "That sounds very nice, thank you very much". I knew about the machinations that had been going on because I'd talked to Tom, and he'd obviously talked to me first. He hadn't gone and said, "Why don't you have her?" without sounding me out to see if I'd like to do it. They were rather grateful that there was somebody that Tom more or less chose himself, that he knew he could get on well with, because he isn't the easiest actor to work with. I mean that in the nicest sort of way: he's actually very demanding, very tricky to work with for some people, and six episodes is a very long audition and you prove at the end of it that you can survive!'

As played by Lalla, the character of Romana mellowed considerably and much of the antagonism between her and the Doctor vanished. The two Time Lords became more of a team with Romana's often outlandish fashion sense, which was an aspect of the character promoted by Lalla. In her first story as Romana, *Destiny of the Daleks*, she ended up wearing a costume that was based on the Doctor's own. 'Everybody involved in the production was asking what sort of person the Doctor would choose as his companion. I said I thought he was such a megalomaniac he'd choose somebody who looked as close to himself as possible, and as I didn't look remotely like him, the only thing I could think of to get anywhere near how he looked was to dress up in his clothes and look like him in that sense.'

Destiny of the Daleks was actually recorded third in sequence and therefore the first story in which Lalla actually performed as Romana was *The Creature from the Pit*. 'I think that shows,' she smiled. 'I was floundering around, I didn't know what to do. I was playing a sort of Mary Tamm *manqué*, really. I was dressed up in floaty gear that Mary looked much better in than I did, I really didn't know what I was doing and I was out of my depth. I felt I was trying to live up to Mary.'

As the series progressed, so Lalla became more confident in the role, even down to discussing costume ideas with the designers. 'Initially the wardrobe department, who were always extremely good and very, very nice to me, would come up and say, "This is what we see you in," and at that stage I really wasn't in a position to object. Later on I became frightfully bossy about what I wore. They'd come in and say, "We see you in a silver lurex catsuit." And I'd say, "Well, I see me in a school uniform can we compromise somewhere?" And that was the way it worked and they were very nice about it. I thought the red riding outfit was rather good. That came about on the principle that Romana

Romana finds herself a captive. The Creature from the Pit.

Top right: Romana with the stowaway Alzarian Adric (Matthew Waterhouse). State of Decay.

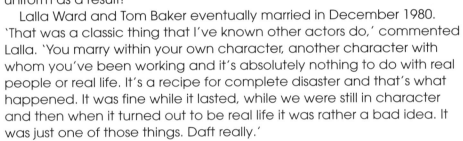

THE TARDIS LOG

Name: Romanadvoratrelundar (Romana).

Origin: Gallifrey.

Likes: Clothes, proving herself smarter than the Doctor, shopping.

Dislikes: Getting dirty, being upstaged by the Doctor.

Lookalikes: Princess Strella of Tara; Princess Astra of Atrios.

Joined the Doctor because: She was assigned to help the Doctor find the six segments of the Key to Time by the White Guardian.

Left the Doctor because: She decided to remain and help the Tharils when the Doctor returned to N-space at the end of *Warriors' Gate.*

General Description: Romana's first incarnation was aristocratic, self-important and argumentative. After her regeneration she became less argumentative and got on a lot better with the Doctor.

Scream Factor: ★★ Although it would not be fitting for a Time Lady to scream, this didn't stop her.

might be the sort of person who, if she lived in England, might go to the Portobello Road and Petticoat Lane in London and accumulate bits and bobs as she went. I rationalised that if you're doing that through time, you could have Victorian riding breeches and an Edwardian jacket and you could muddle it up. It was the only programme where you could get away with wearing a mixture of clothes from different eras.

'Janet Fielding (who played Tegan) later told me that I screwed the costumes up for everyone else as they wore themselves out doing my costumes and by the time she came round, they were sick to death of costumes and so she got stuck in the one uniform as a result!'

Lalla Ward and Tom Baker eventually married in December 1980. 'That was a classic thing that I've known other actors do,' commented Lalla. 'You marry within your own character, another character with whom you've been working and it's absolutely nothing to do with real people or real life. It's a recipe for complete disaster and that's what happened. It was fine while it lasted, while we were still in character and then when it turned out to be real life it was rather a bad idea. It was just one of those things. Daft really.'

Graham Williams moved on from producing *Doctor Who* at the end of the seventeenth season and the task of steering the programme into the eighties fell to the newly appointed producer John Nathan-Turner. Among the many decisions he made in putting together the eighteenth season was the feeling that K-9 had outlived his time in the series, and despite a newspaper campaign launched to save the metal mutt, K-9 left the programme at the end of *Warriors' Gate.*

K-9, however, would not lie down, and returned to television screens in a one-off special, *K-9 and Company,* which also starred Elisabeth Sladen reprising her role as Sarah Jane Smith. In this story, K-9 was a 'Mark 3' model which, in practical terms, meant a new colour scheme (metallic blue), and the addition of a couple of handles to its casing. K-9 continued to work extensively in television, appearing on all manner of children's shows and science-based programmes.

Romana also left the series in *Warriors' Gate.* Despite being summoned to return to Gallifrey, she decided to remain in the smaller universe of Exo-Space and help a race of time-sensitive Tharils free themselves from slavery.

Lalla Ward remembered that her departure from the series was by mutual agreement with Nathan-Turner: 'I went into my last season having had a discussion with John beforehand to decide that halfway through it all, however many episodes it was, I would leave so that the same thing wouldn't happen with my character as had happened with Mary's. We wanted there to be a very definite story that I went out in.'

Looking back on her time with the show, Lalla has no regrets. 'It was a good time, it was a good job. It was extremely frustrating sometimes because you didn't have enough time to do things. It was such a

Adric takes a break. Full Circle.

dreadful schedule, rushing about hither and thither trying to get everything done. It was a time in television when the special effects were very interesting and they were fun to learn about and involved the actors very much , whereas nowadays, I suspect the effects don't involve the cast at all. A lot of *Doctor Who*'s spaceships, let's face it, really came out of cereal packets; I loved that, that's what I thought was lovely about *Doctor Who*. I got the tail end of those days and it subsequently became far more hi-tech: science fiction was suddenly in and everybody was doing it and you had to keep up.

'I liked some of the people who were in it. I loved Tom's obsession with trying his hardest and getting it right, working like a maniac to keep up the standard which he thought was important. It was a good era and it was a lovely job.'

With both Romana and K-9 leaving, producer John Nathan-Turner realised that he needed to introduce a new set of companions who would appeal to the wide range of viewers who comprised *Doctor Who*'s audience. There was another reason for wanting several new faces in the TARDIS and this was that after six years, Tom Baker had decided to step down from playing the Doctor. Because this transition

'The trouble with Adric was that from the beginning he was so damn complicated.'
Matthew Waterhouse

ADRIC

Adric is fifteen, small for his age, wiry and strong. With short straight black hair. His dominating elder brother, Afrus, is the leader of a juvenile street gang on a planet we'll call Yerfillag, and under his tuition Adric has learnt to lie and steal, activities which are the dark side of his natural optimistic brashness and enormous intellectual curiosity.

Adric never fitted into the gang he was pressed into by his brother, partly because of his superior education, and partly because he is a born non-conformist, even among outlaws. When he meets the Doctor, his strong sense of self preservation prompts him to assume an air of subdued innocence and false naivete. Though a disguise, this impersonation reminds us of Adric's very real vulnerability as a young mortal (as opposed to the Time Lords and their all-capable K-9) – vulnerability that is going to play an important part in future adventures.

At the end of the story that introduces Adric, his brother Afrus has given up his life to save the Doctor and Romana. With the last of his family ties broken, Adric stows away in the TARDIS, where he remains undiscovered until the opening of the next story.

The Doctor subsequently shoulders the responsibility for returning Adric to Yerfillag, but what with one thing and another… Meanwhile, Adric's true character is emerging – enquiring, intelligent, but definitely and irritatingly a mendacious magpie. The Doctor's view of his responsibility toward the boy shifts: rather than return him to a planet where he will resume life as a criminal orphan, wouldn't a certain amount of education, reform and expansion of his moral horizon be appropriate…?

BBC Character Outline.

Left: The fifth Doctor (Peter Davison), Adric and Nyssa arrive in 17th century England. The Visitation.

Nyssa (Sarah Sutton) struggles with her step-mother Kassia (Sheila Ruskin). The Keeper of Traken.

Bottom right: Sarah Sutton as Nyssa. Mawdryn Undead.

Opposite: A new team of companions for the fifth Doctor. Tegan (Janet Fielding), Adric (Matthew Waterhouse) and Nyssa (Sarah Sutton).

THE TARDIS LOG

Name: Adric.

Origin: Alzarius.

Likes: Maths, eating and sulking.

Dislikes: Being outsmarted by Tegan and Nyssa. Being turned into a squidgy lump by crashing into the planet Earth. (The dinosaurs probably weren't that keen on it either!)

Joined the Doctor because: He stowed away on the TARDIS.

Left the Doctor because: He was killed trying to stop a freighter from crashing into the Earth.

101 Uses for Adric: No. 1: as an interesting wall decoration in Castrovalva.

General Description: Total wimp. From his pudding bowl hair cut (the kind of cut that parents force on their kids) to his love of maths, at school he must have been the class nerd.

Scream Factor: ★ More of a whimperer than a screamer.

was possibly the greatest change the series had seen since the departure of the first Doctor in 1966, it was felt that familiar faces were needed to provide audience continuity over the change of Doctor.

The first of the new team to be devised was Adric, an alien youth whom the Doctor first encountered on the planet Alzarius in Exo-Space, and whom Nathan-Turner described to the press as a 'cosmic Artful Dodger'. Adric was introduced as early as possible to try and ensure that he was established before the climax of the season.

When it came to cast the part, Nathan-Turner has admitted that he chose novice actor Matthew Waterhouse because he 'was not the type to be found on the front of chocolate boxes!' The idea was to present Adric as a young roguish roughneck, with enough charm to offset the more criminal tendencies of his upbringing.

One of the problems from Matthew Waterhouse's point of view was that the character of Adric changed from story to story. 'As far as I'm concerned, in each four episodes he was a new individual. Every time I established a kind of gut feeling about him, about what he should do and think, it was contradicted in the next script.' This lack of any development, and indeed, Waterhouse's admitted approach to the part, was evident in the transmitted episodes.

In Adric's debut story, Full Circle, he was introduced as a child genius, someone who had been awarded a gold star for mathematical excellence, yet he craved the recognition of his peers, and especially his brother, Varsh. When his brother was killed, Adric began to realise that his future life would not be with those who had brought him up. Thus he stowed away on board the TARDIS and left with the Doctor instead. Adric was an Alzarian, a race encountered by the Doctor in E-Space. The Alzarians had great recuperative powers and adapted quickly to planetary changes. In fact, Adric's people thought they were Terradonians, not realising that the original Terradonians had been wiped out by the Alzarian marshmen, who had rapidly evolved and adapted to become like those they had killed.

Following this imaginative introduction, thereafter Adric did very little except look moody. The writers seemed unsure of how to handle the character and what part he could usefully play in their stories. Thus there was the inclusion of scenes like that in The Visitation where Adric tripped (somewhat unconvincingly) and sprained his ankle while running through the woods.

About the only aspect of Adric's background that was picked up in subsequent scripts was that as an Alzarian, he healed very quickly – therefore, for example, his ankle was better within a few

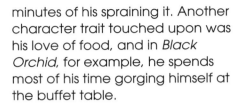

Above right: Sarah Sutton.

Opposite: Nyssa had a change of costume for Snakedance.

Sarah Sutton with Mark Strickson, who took on the role of Turlough.

minutes of his spraining it. Another character trait touched upon was his love of food, and in *Black Orchid*, for example, he spends most of his time gorging himself at the buffet table.

The second of the new companions, Nyssa, was originally created for a single story, *The Keeper of Traken*.

The potential of Johnny Byrne's character was spotted by the production team as a possible regular who would help bridge the gap between Tom Baker's departure and Peter Davison's arrival as the fifth Doctor. Johnny Byrne recalled that the decision to include Nyssa as a regular character was made after he had delivered the completed scripts for the story. He was asked to provide a character outline sheet once the decision had been taken. Byrne recalled that the society from which Nyssa originated was 'hi-tech medieval, mixing the scientific and the spiritual' and that Nyssa herself embodied these themes also. 'She had an almost prophetic sense of destiny,' he explained. 'All the time thereafter, she believed that she should have been there with her people to share whatever fate had in store for them. The thing that kept her going was that her father had sacrificed himself for her, and she was fighting the feeling that she should have suffered herself. Survivor guilt is a fairly common psychological problem.

'The actual name was a contraction of one of two twins called Nerissa and Fanny whom I knew, but the character came out of the situation I had in the plot. I wanted someone who could relate to Adric in a way. I wanted some kind of representative of a younger feeling about this world I had created and it went through a number of changes as it developed.'

The part of Nyssa went to a young actress called Sarah Sutton, best known for her starring role in a children's serial called *The Moon Stallion*. Sutton was initially hired by director John Black for *The Keeper of Traken* but with an option on her services if the production team were happy with her performance.

Although extremely bright, Nyssa was an innocent character. She had grown up in the protective atmosphere of the Traken Union, where those with evil intent were immediately calcified when they set foot on the planet. However, the Master managed to overcome this problem and wreaked havoc on her home world, eventually killing her father and taking his body as well as causing the eventual destruction of the planet in *Logopolis*. The now-orphaned Nyssa joined the other companions in the TARDIS.

Nyssa proved to be the balance between Tegan's

'I think what was quite nice about Nyssa was that she started out relatively strongly. Companions all start with good intentions but after a few episodes inevitably they get back into the same old mould. It's very difficult to maintain anything you start off with, but Nyssa didn't do too badly. I actually did like Nyssa very much.'

Sarah Sutton

NYSSA

Nyssa is the daughter of Tremas, First Scientist and Consul of the Empire of Traken. Tremas is now dead at the hand of the Master, who has commandeered his cadaver by way of a thirteenth regeneration. She is eighteen, of noble birth; an attractive young girl with values and skills deeply rooted in her Traken past. Tutored by her father in the advanced sciences, she is already a skilled apprentice in bioelectronics, a discipline in which her people excelled.

Nyssa is an open young woman. Idealistic and pragmatic by turn, she has an abiding belief in the essential goodness of all things, which sometimes blinds her to the less overt manifestations of evil. For example, in meeting the Master for the first time in his new guise she has mistaken him for her father, only being rescued from his clutches by the intervention of Adric and the Doctor. A threat once visible, however, brings out all that is best in Nyssa: calm assessment, lightning judgement, and nicely judged action.

Nyssa's aristocratic background sometimes leaves her oblivious to the simpler needs of others, and occasionally prevents her from seeing the funny side of situations. Adric, an orphan like her, is very fond of Nyssa, but at times her innocence, seriousness and inability to compromise seem to him like deliberate stubbornness.

The Doctor feels, irrationally, a sense of responsibility for the death of her father, but has too much respect for her individuality to see himself as any kind of substitute. He appears, in his offhand way, to enjoy having her around and being in some small part a force in her spiritual development. He would never allow it to be seen that deep, deep down inside the presence of all these young people in the TARDIS is very wearing!

BBC Character Outline.
*Johnny Byrne, John Nathan-Turner, Christopher H. Bidmead.
30 Oct 1980.*

Tegan (Janet Fielding) and Nyssa in the TARDIS laboratory. Terminus.

over-emotive nature and Adric's hot temper. She always remained cool under pressure and worked out situations logically. Her dress sense also changed dramatically, from a rather sombre brown costume in *The Keeper of Traken* to the more colourful outfits worn in *Arc of Infinity*, *Snakedance* and *Mawdryn Undead*. 'Poor Janet's costumes were so impractical but I was lucky – I was in trousers for a while. John (Nathan-Turner) told me that he'd had a lot of complaining letters, all saying: "Where have Nyssa's legs gone?" when I went from my original skirt to trousers, so that's why I went back into a shorter skirt.'

With three companions in the TARDIS, writers found it extremely hard to split up their stories in such a way that each character could be given enough to do. This often led to some characters getting little development throughout the season until a story that featured them more heavily came along. In the case of *Kinda*, Nyssa was written out of the story (she was in an induced sleep in the TARDIS) to allow greater development of the Mara-Tegan storyline.

Completing the line-up of companions to carry the viewers through the regeneration of Tom Baker into Peter Davison was Tegan. When formulating ideas for the Doctor's new companions, Nathan-Turner originally felt that Tegan might not stay with the Doctor for very long, hence the initial character breakdowns and casting requirements specified that she was only in three stories. Ultimately, however, Nathan-Turner decided that Tegan should become a more permanent member of the TARDIS crew.

The initial character was sketched out by Nathan-Turner and then

further developed by script editor Christopher H. Bidmead, who had taken over at the start of the eighteenth season. As Nathan-Turner recalls, he was unsure of the character's name. 'It was to be either Tegan (a friend's niece in Sydney is called Tegan), or Jovanka (the name of President Tito's widow), and at the top of the paper I had written: "Tegan – Jovanka". Christopher assumed that Jovanka was her surname-to-be, rather than an alternative, and Tegan Jovanka was born.'

Following the initial outline, a slightly amended version was used in the *Doctor Who* 'notes', a guide for writers which encompassed all the regular elements of the series. In this revised version, dated 14 November 1980, the following paragraph concerning the character's background was added:

On her father's farm near Brisbane, which has its own plane, she became very keen on flying and everything to do with the air. When the opportunity arose for her to do an air stewardess's course in England, she came over to stay with her Aunt Vanessa.

The revised document later referred to 'a particularly nasty battle of wits with the Master' but otherwise was as originally drafted.

Tegan proved very popular with viewers and the actress who played her, Janet Fielding, put this down to attitude. 'I think it's because she

Tegan and the Doctor attend captain Wrack's party. Enlightenment.

Above left: Janet Fielding pictured in 1978.

Tegan, the Doctor and Turlough (Mark Strickson). Warriors of the Deep.

THE TARDIS LOG

Name: Tegan Jovanka.

Occupation: Trainee Air Stewardess.

Origin: Earth, Australia, 1980s.

Likes: Whining, whingeing, moaning, complaining… need I go on'

Dislikes: Almost everything.

Favourite Swear Word: Rabbits!

Joined the Doctor because: She mistook the TARDIS for a real police box (in 1981? Come on, even Tegan must have realised it was twenty years out of date).

Left the Doctor because: She had enough of all the murder and mayhem that tends to go with being a companion of the Doctor.

Companion most likely to: Be Prime Minister.

General Description: Gorgeous brunette with a huge attitude problem. A request for a drink from this stewardess would probably have been answered with a smack in the mouth. She dressed to kill and then wondered why everyone around her died. Once described herself as 'a mouth on legs'.

TEGAN JOVANKA

Tegan is twenty–one, an attractive and intelligent Australian trainee air stewardess, whose brash confidence in her own abilities actually conceals inner insecurity, a state of affairs that becomes clear in moments of stress.

On her way to her first real flight she accidentally blunders into the TARDIS and thus finds herself being inadvertently abducted by the Doctor. Characteristically her inner bewilderment at the new situation in which she finds herself causes her to assume an attitude of overweening self–assertion, and she begins to take charge of the Doctor and Adric.

During the course of three stories, Tegan's superficial self–assurance will build until it becomes a real problem for the other two occupants of the TARDIS, and it will need drastic action on the part of the Doctor to put things to rights and show her the error of her ways. She may or may not continue with the Doctor thereafter.

BBC Character Outline.
John Nathan–Turner and
Christopher H. Bidmead.
1 August 1980.

Opposite: Janet Fielding.

Tegan, wearing the Doctor's dream-inhibiting device, enters the fortune teller's (Hillary Sesta) tent. Snakedance.

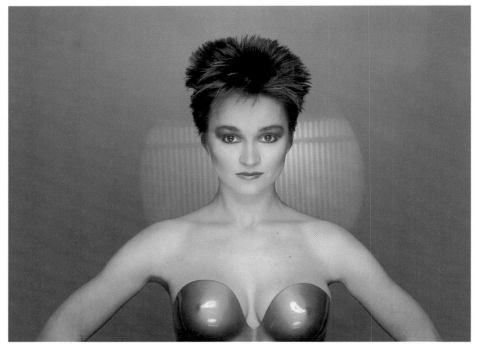

Janet Fielding in 1982.

was so bolshie! She was quite aggressive although this was naturally toned down as we went along.'

The first of the companions to be written out was Adric. John Nathan-Turner had decided that Adric was to be killed, thus leaving in a dramatic and emotional way. This fate had only befallen two of the Doctor's companions in the past (Katarina and Sara Kingdom) but neither of those companions had been with the Doctor for very long. This was to be the first time a long-running companion had been killed.

John Nathan-Turner recalled that Matthew Waterhouse refused to speak to him for almost two weeks after he read the script in which Adric died. The fact of Adric's departure from the series was, as Waterhouse explained, 'a kind of joint decision. As far as I was concerned, everything sort of died on me. I'd done all I could'.

In the script, Adric was left on board a freighter which was rushing towards a fatal impact with the Earth and he used his mathematical skills to try and decipher the codes on a guidance device left by the Cybermen. He managed to crack two of the codes, making the freighter slip backwards through time, but the third eluded him. A rogue Cyberman destroyed the console on which he was working and he could do nothing but stand and gaze at the approaching Earth, clutching his tribal belt given to him by his dead brother, Varsh. This was a very moving and effective departure for Adric, and a very brave step for the production team to have taken.

Matthew Waterhouse returned twice more to the series to reprise his character. Once was in *Time Flight,* the story that immediately followed *Earthshock,* when an image of Adric was conjured to try and prevent Nyssa and Tegan from penetrating the inner sanctum of the Xeraphin; the second time was at the end of *The Caves of Androzani* ,where the regenerating Doctor sees and hears his

'I always thought of Tegan as Lucy (from Charles Schultz's *Peanuts* cartoons) in space.'

Janet Fielding

companions urging him to live.

Following Adric's departure, the male companion was not reinstated immediately. Instead, several stories passed before Turlough was introduced as a new face in the TARDIS. As a concept, Turlough was to be like no other companion. He was secretly working against the Doctor rather than assisting him and was merely a pawn in the schemes of the Black Guardian who was plotting his revenge against the Doctor. The idea of an 'evil' companion was first mooted at a script conference held by script editor Eric Saward and it was decided that Turlough would not be wholeheartedly evil, but more of an amoral character who reacted unpredictably at moments of stress and tension. The script which was originally to have introduced Turlough was Pat Mills' *Song of the Space Whale*, which was in development towards the end of 1981. This script fell through, however, and ultimately it was left up to Peter Grimwade to introduce the character in *Mawdryn Undead*, commissioned in May 1982.

Turlough jokes with the sailors working on the Eternals' racing yacht. Enlightenment.

Opposite: Turlough (Mark Strickson), an exiled alien who made a deal with the Black Guardian to kill the Doctor in return for his freedom. Enlightenment. To enhance Turlough's alien nature, the BBC Make-up department provided an unusual set of eyebrows and also dyed Mark strickson's hair red as his natural colour was felt to be too close to that of Peter Davison.

The many expressions of Turlough's shady character. Enlightenment.

'I brought in the element of using a past companion,' recalled Grimwade in 1988. 'I originally thought I'd go right back to the beginning and have Ian, the teacher, and I was quite pleased with the structure of that. The moment I thought about bringing a companion back from the past, I thought about Ian, which gave me a school. Then I sort of got the feel of a dreadful kind of minor public school and I characterised the setting and this boy, so that when Turlough came along, I said he'd have to be at the school. Then, in discussions with Eric (Saward), and as we were bringing in the Brigadier, we saw it was all getting very complicated.'

Turlough's past was initially shrouded in mystery. During his first story, *Mawdryn Undead*, he revealed that he had been forced into exile at Brendon School on Earth. Why he was an exile and from which planet he originated, however, was not explained until his final story, *Planet of Fire*.

'In a show supposed to be geared to pace like *Doctor Who*, and with more than one regular cast member, there wasn't room for such a diverse, ambiguous character as Turlough.'

Mark Strickson

Turlough and Tegan's grandfather, Andrew Verney (Frederick Hall) in the church's crypt. The Awakening.

TURLOUGH

A 20-year-old blond skinny youth, whom the Doctor first meets on a planet, on which he has lived as long as he can remember.

He is blunt, occasionally aggressive, but has an engaging personality. Despite his bluntness, he's chirpy and ever-ready with an amusing quip. We will eventually discover he is in the employ (or under the control) of the Black Guardian.

Turlough wishes to join forces with the Doctor in order to gain access to the TARDIS.

In Turlough's first story, during which the Doctor will save his life, we will be sure that the youth is worthy of joining the Doctor – this will be achieved at the end of the four parter, though Nyssa and Tegan will be suspicious of the boy's motives and surprised at the Doctor's blindness to Turlough's deviousness.

In the second story, Turlough will attempt to engineer the downfall of the Doctor. The Doctor and companions will not realise Turlough's involvement, though the audience, of course, will. Needless to say the plan fails, and we end this story with the Doctor's suspicions aroused as to Turlough's credibility.

In Turlough's third story, the Doctor will have his suspicions confirmed and once again foil the boy's schemes, and dispense with the Black Guardian.

Turlough may or may not continue with the Doctor, but whichever is decided, Turlough will turn over a new leaf (perhaps!).

BBC Character Outline.
John Nathan-Turner. 15 May 1981.

Actor Mark Strickson was cast to play the part by John Nathan-Turner. 'I went along for an interview and read-through,' explained Mark, 'not thinking for a moment that I'd actually get it. So many people in our profession are chasing very few jobs and you go along to loads of interviews largely knowing you're unlikely to get the job.' At the same time as Mark was offered the role of Turlough, he was also offered the role of a regular character on *Angels*. He chose the *Doctor Who* part as he had not enjoyed his previous work on *Angels*.

Both Nyssa and Tegan were initially extremely wary of the newcomer to the TARDIS. Although the Doctor apparently failed to see Turlough's untrustworthy nature, Tegan was quickly convinced that he was up to no good. The first three stories in which Turlough appeared formed a trilogy covering the Black Guardian's plot to destroy the Time Lord. In the last of the three stories, *Enlightenment*, Turlough refused to kill the Doctor despite the Guardian's threats and the tie between them was finally broken.

Nyssa left in the second of the three Black Guardian stories, *Terminus*. With her character pretty well established as a caring and thoughtful individual, it seemed right that she should decide to devote time to developing a cure for a hideous leprosy-like illness known as Lazar disease. Sarah Sutton remembered her departure from the series: 'I think her last story, instead of Nyssa just fizzling out, was quite strong. I was lucky with that because some last stories can be a bit of a wet fish.'

Unfortunately for Turlough, the end of *Enlightenment* marked a slight change of emphasis back to the Doctor and Tegan. After his double nature was revealed and effectively nullified by the defeat of the Black Guardian, Turlough started to fall into the more traditional companion role, but throughout the period, Strickson maintained a believability in the character that went further than the scripts. More information was discovered about his background in *Frontios*, where it was revealed

After summoning a ship from his home world of Trion to rescue the people on Sarn, Turlough finds he has been pardoned and can return home. Planet of Fire.

The Doctor and the Master use their mental powers to battle for the control of Kamelion. The King's Demons.

THE TARDIS LOG

Name: Vizlor Turlough.

Rank: Junior Ensign Commander.

Origin: Trion.

Likes: Being underhanded and sneaky, crashing classic cars, arguing with Tegan.

Dislikes: English public school, the Black Guardian, Tractators.

Joined the Doctor because: Made a deal with the Black Guardian to help him kill the Doctor.

Left the Doctor because: He was allowed to return to his home planet of Trion.

Companion most likely to: win an eyebrow-twitching contest.

General Description: An extremely suspicious character, forever wandering off on his own and muttering into a small glowing crystal. A disaster at parties. Not to be trusted.

that Turlough's home planet, unnamed at this point, also suffered from an infestation of the grub-like Tractators. Turlough recalled this racial memory from deep in his subconscious while still in shock after his initial realisation that the Tractators were present on the planet Frontios. Following *Terminus*, where Tegan and Turlough were forced to put up with each other's company for most of the story, Tegan's attitude towards him mellowed slightly, and his calm and calculating manner balanced her more fiery reactions.

The Kamelion android on display at the 1983 Longleat convention.

One of the strangest creatures with whom the Doctor has travelled was a shape-shifting android called Kamelion. This computer-controlled, sound activated, animated robot had been created by Mike Power and Chris Padmore and was owned by CP Cybernetics, a company specialising in animated displays and microprocessor systems. CPC was run by Chris Padmore, a colleague of Richard Gregory, whose Imagineering company had manufactured several props and costumes for *Doctor Who* including the Terileptils for *The Visitation* and the newly redesigned Cybermen for *Earthshock*.

It was during the recording of *Earthshock* that Gregory approached John Nathan-Turner to see whether he would be interested in featuring the robot in the series. Nathan-Turner was sufficiently intrigued to ask Gregory, Padmore and Power to bring the then unnamed android to the studios for a demonstration.

A few weeks later, script editor Eric Saward, writer Terence Dudley and John Nathan-Turner travelled to Imagineering's Oxford workshop to see the robot again. Dudley christened the android Kamelion and was given the task of writing a two-part story, initially called *The Android*, around the metal creation.

'It was rather weird sitting in rehearsals when they brought this thing in, as I was sitting there reading my newspaper and I heard my voice emanating from the other side of the room out of this strange creature.'

Gerald Flood

Gerald Flood as Kamelion/King John. The King's Demons.

Kamelion, affected by Peri's thoughts, takes on the appearance of her step-father Howard (Dallas Adams). Planet of Fire.

According to Dudley's script, Kamelion was a tool of the Master, who had discovered the android as he was attempting to escape Xeriphas, the planet on which he had been left by the Doctor at the conclusion of their last encounter in *Time Flight*. Kamelion was a weapon created by an earlier invader of the planet. It was able to change shape and personality through the thoughts of those that controlled it and the Master employed his superior mind-control to use the android first to escape from Xeriphas, and then to travel to Earth in an attempt to wreck the signing of the Magna Carta in the year 1215. The Doctor used his own mental powers to release Kamelion from the Master's control. The Master's plans were foiled and the Doctor gained the android as a travelling companion when he realised that the creature had a mind of its own when not subjected to the control of others.

Veteran actor Gerald Flood was hired to play the voice of Kamelion as well as playing King John (whom the android was impersonating) in the final version of the story, retitled *The King's Demons*.

Despite the best intentions of the production team, Kamelion's limitations quickly became apparent. Programming in the required speech and movement reportedly took over nine days to complete, and the robot was unable to walk, leaving it somewhat static and uninteresting. There were also problems with the BBC unions, in that Kamelion needed a power supply and, under union rules, only an electrician could plug the robot in.

Another problem was that soon after agreement had been reached to include the robot in the series, Mike Power was involved in a boating accident and subsequently died. Wheras Padmore had created the hardware for the creature, Power had been working on the computer software, and he had not left sufficient notes for anyone else to pick up his work.

As a result of these problems, although Kamelion left with the Doctor at the end of the story, the android did not appear in the following five stories. It was intended to be seen briefly at the start of *The Awakening*, being voiced by Mark Strickson and Peter Davison. This was among those scenes edited out when the story was found to be running over length.

Towards the end of the 21st season, with both Mark Strickson and Peter Davison leaving their respective roles, Janet Fielding also decided that the time was right to move on. She felt that she had done three years and that perhaps it was time to leave. 'I couldn't – wouldn't – have chosen to do any more. That was it,' she explained.

A decision was taken to stage an emotional farewell to Tegan and an abrupt departure was included following a battle in *Resurrection of the Daleks*, where Tegan became sickened by the number of deaths she had witnessed in the Doctor's company. She ran from the warehouse in which the TARDIS had materialised, and the last shot we witnessed, she watched tearfully as the TARDIS dematerialised before her eyes.

Turlough was also written out of the series in the closing stages of the 21st season. In his final story, *Planet of Fire*, written by Peter Grimwade, who had also scripted his introductory story, we discovered that Turlough's first name was Vizlor, and that he was an exile from a civil war

on his home planet of Trion. After discovering equipment on the dying planet of Sarn, which he believed came from his father's spaceship, he realised that one of those already on the planet, Malkon, was in fact his younger brother. Together they found the wreck of their father's ship and used the radio equipment inside to place an emergency call to Trion to rescue those living on Sarn. Turlough explained that his mother was killed in a civil war on Trion, and that his father and younger brother were sentenced to exile on Sarn. Turlough had been sent to public school on Earth, watched over by a Trion operative posing as a London solicitor. Luckily for Turlough, when the Trion rescue ship arrived on Sarn, its captain revealed that there had been an amnesty granted to all political prisoners and that Turlough was therefore able to return home.

The means of writing out Turlough was, according to Grimwade, 'something that had come to me in embryo when I'd written *Mawdryn Undead*. I had, for my own peace of mind, to give myself a reason for Turlough to be there in the first place, so I just built on that.'

Mark Strickson recalled that his departure from the programme was by mutual agreement with the production team. 'We came to a very sensible and amicable agreement that, with a whole new team coming in, and with Turlough having done all he could usefully do, it was time he should go.'

Kamelion was also written out in *Planet of Fire*, and this final appearance was only the second story in which the creature had appeared. Because of continuing problems with programming the android, and the fact that much of the story was recorded on location in Lanzarote, Kamelion's shape-shifting ability was used to allow the android to be played by both Anthony Ainley (also playing the Master in the story) and Dallas Adams (who was also playing Peri's stepfather, Howard Foster). The robot's appearance in its true form was reduced to a number of studio scenes at the beginning and end of the story.

Kamelion had been taken over by the Master once more and used to take the TARDIS to the dying planet Sarn where, at the story's conclusion, he was once again freed from the Master's control. The creature appeared to be malfunctioning, however, and was more of a continued threat to the Doctor than a useful ally; he asked the Doctor to release him by ending his existence using the Master's tissue compression eliminator, and the Doctor complied. This was the only example in *Doctor Who* of the Doctor directly 'killing' one of his companions. Ultimately Kamelion was a case of modern technology not quite being up to the requirements of the futuristic *Doctor Who* universe, although the creature will remain one of the strangest and most alien of the Doctor's companions.

THE TARDIS LOG

Name: Kamelion.

Origin: From an unnamed planet, but found on Xeriphas by the Master.

Occupation: Weapon of war.

Likes: Rory Bremner, Mike Yarwood, Monet and other impressionists.

Dislikes: Keeping up appearances.

Lookalikes: Almost anything and anyone.

Joined the Doctor because: The Doctor hustled him into the TARDIS thinking he was Tegan.

Left the Doctor because: Fed up of being used by the Master, he asked the Doctor to kill him. Well, you would, wouldn't you?

General Description: One minute a shop dummy painted silver, the next... who knows?

Top left: Turlough takes a stroll. Mawdryn Undead.

The true appearance of the shape-changing android Kamelion. The King's Demons.

A SIGN OF THE EIGHTIES

Peri's body is stolen by Kiv. The Trial of a Time Lord.

Opposite: Nicola Bryant pictured in 1983.

Below right: Peri transforms into a bird. Vengeance on Varos.

THE TARDIS LOG

Name: Perpugilliam (Peri) Brown.

Occupation: Student.

Origin: Earth, America (according to her passport, Peri was born on 15 November, and currently resides at 45th Street, St Michelle, Pasadena, California), 1980s.

Likes: Independence, travel, botany, unsuitable clothes.

Dislikes: Being locked up, having demented suitors, her stepfather, very short haircuts.

Joined the Doctor because: She was bored by the prospect of returning to Earth and asked the Doctor if he would show her the Universe.

Left the Doctor because: She was either a) married to King Yrcanos or b) killed when her brain was overprinted with that of the Mentor Sil. It depends on what you believe.

General Description: Sexy, sassy and American to the hilt. Peri suffered more than most from aliens coveting her person.

Companion most likely to: Change her name at the first opportunity.

Scream Factor: ★★★★ Another companion with a great pair of lungs.

When Janet Fielding's Tegan and Mark Strickson's Turlough left almost simultaneously, the production team decided to break with tradition. John Nathan-Turner explained that 'the decision to try one solitary companion with the Doctor was an attempt to echo the Pertwee-Jo relationship of the seventies, which had been so successful.'

As script editor Eric Saward recalled, it was Nathan-Turner's decision to make the new companion, Peri, an American. 'John wanted an American,' he said, 'and his brief was simply that: an American.' Nathan-Turner explained that it was the fact that *Doctor Who* was British that attracted a world-wide audience, and after the undoubted success of Tegan – another non-British Earth companion – he wanted an American travelling in the TARDIS.

Following auditions, Nathan-Turner eventually chose an actress straight out of drama school, Nicola Bryant, to play the part, despite the fact that she wasn't American at all.

'When I auditioned for *Doctor Who*, John had no idea that I was not really American,' explained Nicola. 'I do have dual nationality through my marriage and also my room-mate at boarding school was from New York so I had picked up her accent. I had been playing an American in *No, No, Nanette* and an agent, Terry Carney, who came in to see it, assumed that I was American. He called me up and asked me to go and audition for *Doctor Who*. He didn't want to take on someone new out of drama school unless they had a job, so this was in his interest as well as mine. I told him that I wasn't strictly American but he told me to be American anyway. So I did and I thought that if they weren't happy with my American-ness, they'd just reject me. There was someone from Denver at the office and I thought that if I convinced him then I was doing all right.

'I went through several auditions until it finally got down to a choice between me and one other actress. They decided that they wanted me but then of course I had to get my Equity card, because they couldn't let me have the part unless I was a member of the union. I had to get all my friends together and do cabaret work around some clubs to gain enough work experience to qualify for membership.'

Nicola had envisaged Peri herself as being 'a naïve innocent: quite a spunky kid, but not really experienced, having had a pretty sheltered upbringing, with a domineering mother and a stepfather who wasn't exactly a bundle of laughs'.

What happened in practice was that particular character traits were

Peri awaits her grisly fate, to be transformed into a half-human, half-Morlox monster. Timelash.

Opposite: Nicola Bryant pictured in 1986.

Below right: Peri is forced to watch the apparent death of the Doctor in the punishment dome. Vengeance on Varos.

PERI

Perpugilliam (Peri for short) Brown is a wealthy 18-year-old American student studying Botany. She has long blonde hair which complements her attractive looks. She does not suffer fools gladly and her most charming attribute is an acute sense of humour.

We meet Peri for the first time, while she is on holiday in whichever country we decide to film next season's foreign story.

Peri's mother, Janine, has remarried a man Peri dislikes – Howard. Peri still treasures the memory of her father who died when Peri was 13, particularly as her mother appears to care more for Howard's three children than for Peri herself. It is because of her respect for her father that Peri thinks so highly of the Doctor – to some extent the Doctor replaces the gap in Peri's life. When he died he was of the same age as the Doctor appears now. This never develops further than admiration and close friendship. Peri is the kind of girl who is popular – not just because of her looks, but because her warmth and sense of fun make her appeal to people of all ages.

BBC Character Outline.
John Nathan-Turner, Eric Saward

either emphasised or lost by successive writers on the show, a lack of continuity which Nicola found very off-putting: 'I would suddenly find that a writer had highlighted one particular aspect, which might be one which I had never seen as a major part of the character anyway.'

Peri's outfits were both eye-catching and colourful, generally consisting of figure-hugging shorts and skin-tight leotards. This element of the characterisation, developed to appeal to the tabloid press and any males who cared to tune in, came about, according to Nathan-Turner, because of the clothes Nicola chose to wear to her first photo-call. 'I thought she looked so stunning,' he explained, 'that I asked our costume designers to echo Nicola's own clothes!'

'I was asked to bring several outfits along for the photo-call,' said Nicola, 'and "short and very fitting" was the description I was given. I never wore short skirts and clingy-fitting tops myself – all I possessed was a pair of shorts and a leotard. I asked John if this would be okay and he said, "Great!" Unfortunately, he liked it so much that we got stuck with it.'

Over the course of two stories, Peri quickly established an amicable rapport with the fifth Doctor, but all this was to change as Peter Davison left and Colin Baker joined as the sixth incarnation of the Time Lord. In an attempt to emphasise the instability of the latest regeneration, the production team chose to make the sixth Doctor initially very unstable and unpredictable, with a wild temper and a tendency towards violence. Peri found herself faced with a manic personality in the TARDIS, who in turn complimented and then tried to strangle her.

Peri's character degenerated after this initial period into something of a moaner, always whinging about where they were going and what they were doing. Following the hiatus between the 22nd and the 23rd seasons, the characters of both Peri and the Doctor had mellowed: the actors concerned had decided that they could not go on being at each other's throats for any longer. Instead, there was a respectful acceptance of each other's company – at least for the first segment of *The Trial of a Time Lord*. For the second segment, the Doctor was again acting erratically and, ultimately, Peri was written out in a gruesome manner.

The method of her departure was prompted by a desire by all concerned not to marry her off. In the second segment of *The Trial of a Time Lord*, Peri's brain was replaced by that of the Mentor Kiv, and the final scenes of a bald-headed Peri, speaking in Kiv's harsh tones about how wonderful this new body was, were very effective.

There was, however, much controversy over Peri's exit. As that segment of the Doctor's trial had been tampered with by the Valeyard in the Matrix on Gallifrey, we were left uncertain as to what was real and what had been faked. At the conclusion of the trial, the Inquisitor calmed the Doctor's fears about Peri

'I had a horrible time with the press.'

Nicola Bryant

MEL

Melanie is scintillating, fascinating and irritating. She has a mane of red hair, fierce blue eyes and freckles. She is twenty-one years old and a computer programmer from Pease Pottage, Sussex.

In 1986, when the Master attempted a massive computer fraud involving all the banking houses in the world, Melanie joined forces with the Doctor, helping to defeat the Master's dastardly plan, and has now been with him for some three months (in Earth time).

Melanie is one of those annoying young ladies who is a 'feminist' at all times, except at moments of great stress, when she relies heavily on playing the hard-done-by, down-trodden, crocodile-teared female.

She is heavily into aerobics and health food. She considers the Doctor overweight and in need of regular Jane Fonda-type movement lessons, although the Doctor insists he gets quite enough exercise dashing around the Galaxy, defeating evil. She often attempts to force health-giving vitamin-enriched food on the Doctor (muesli, raw carrots etc.), which may provide useful comic relief.

Despite her feminist attitudes, she appears to attempt to stabilise the Doctor's hitherto, in her opinion, unhealthy and irrational way of life.

She has a strong sense of humour and is often heard singing in the TARDIS, much to the annoyance of the Doctor.

Although the Doctor is ferociously fond of Melanie, who prefers to be known as Mel (well, she would, wouldn't she?), he resists all attempts to stabilise his existence.

Melanie is the first Earth-UK companion for twelve years. We shall soon see why.

Mel screams well and runs down corridors with elan. (Despite being a computer programmer, Melanie cannot operate the TARDIS. On the odd occasion that she tries, disaster ensues.)

BBC Character Outline.
John Nathan-Turner. July 1985.

by explaining that she eventually married the Krontep warlord Yrcanos and was now living as his queen. This was an ironic end to the character, considering that no one wanted to see Peri married off in the first place.

Nicola Bryant decided to leave *Doctor Who* simply because she, like several of the people who had played companions before her, felt that three years working on one show was enough. 'As an actor I had to say, "Right, okay, I'm going to get out there and see what else there is." I was happy to do so in that I felt that I wanted to go and do something else, but sad to be leaving such a nice bunch of people behind.'

Unlike all the other companions of the Doctor, there were no auditions for the part of computer programmer Mel Bush (although the surname was never used on screen). John Nathan-Turner had drafted the character outline in July 1985, and at Christmas that year he was having a meeting with Colin Baker's agent Barry Burnett, who also handled Bonnie Langford, when he realised that Langford fitted his character outline perfectly. He suggested to Burnett that Langford would be ideal, she was approached and agreed to do it.

This story, as related by John Nathan-Turner, is at odds with script editor Eric Saward's later recollection that Nathan-Turner had wanted Langford in the programme all along and had devised the outline accordingly. 'John said, "I was thinking of a new companion the other day," recalled Saward when asked about the circumstances of Langford's casting in 1993. 'I said, "Oh yes, who?" He said, "Well, I want her to have red hair." So I said, "Oh yes, why's that?" He said, "Well, because I think that she must have red hair." So I said, "Fine, have you got anyone in mind?" And he said, "There's only one person I can think of who has got beautiful red hair: Bonnie Langford." '

Bonnie Langford had been a child actress 'discovered' by Hughie Green's popular *Opportunity Knocks* talent show on television. She was perhaps best known at the time for her performance as the precocious and obnoxious Violet Elizabeth Bott in a television adaptation of Richmal Crompton's *Just William* stories, and this popular typecast view of the actress was uppermost in people's minds.

Langford recalled that she had met John Nathan-Turner some time before her eventual casting, at a restaurant called Joe Allen's. 'I'd been chatting to Faith Brown, who'd just been in a *Doctor Who*, and I said, "I'd love to do one of those, that'd be fun," and obviously some seeds were sown there. Literally a year or so later, I got this phone call from my agent, saying John Nathan-Turner would like me to meet him in his office.

'I went down there and he showed me this sort of character

Mel and the Doctor (Sylvester McCoy) encounter the Tollmaster (Ken Dodd). Delta and the Bannermen.

analysis of Mel and he said, "What do you think?" I said, "That's a nice character, sounds fun." So he said, "Well, would you like to do it?" And that was it, really.'

Following Langford's acceptance of the role, in January 1986 Saward drafted a short piece for her to perform in order for the production team and writers to get a feel for her performance as soon as possible.

The other aspect that set Mel aside from the other companions was that, with the sole exception of the Doctor's granddaughter, Susan, she was not seen to join the Doctor during the televised adventures.

We were first introduced to her in the penultimate segment of *The Trial of a Time Lord* where the Doctor was introducing an adventure from his future as part of his defence. Mel was a bouncy, red-headed health-and-fitness enthusiast. When presented with gymnasium facilities on the *Hyperion III* space liner, she used them. She also tried to get the Doctor to do some exercise and to drink carrot juice, a substance about which he was less than enthusiastic. She was inquisitive, intelligent and actually provided a good match for the sometimes bombastic and self-assured persona of the sixth Doctor.

As the epic trial drew to a conclusion, Mel was summoned and brought to the trial ship by the Master, and at the end of the story she left with the Doctor. It is debatable, therefore, whether this was Mel's 'first' – chronologically for the Doctor – meeting with him, and that the Master actually made the fact of the Doctor's future travels with Mel happen in the first place.

When Bonnie Langford was revealed as the Doctor's newest companion, there was an immediate reaction, both from the popular press and the many fans of the programme. The press were very positive, and the news coverage was both widespread and impressive. The fan reaction was less enthusiastic from some quarters, with the decision being criticised even before she had been seen in the role.

After only 20 episodes, Bonnie decided to move on from the series because she felt that she had done all she could. 'There are limitations to the part and I don't want to go on doing it forever. You keep thinking, "People are going to be so sick of this loon with the red hair running round saying 'Doctor!'" ' and I don't want the character to be like that. I don't want to be just a funny old sidekick.'

Thus Mel decided to switch her loyalties from the Doctor to the intergalactic rogue Sabalom Glitz when they bumped into him on the planet Svartos in the story *Dragonfire*. Mel went with Glitz to try and keep him on the straight and narrow, while the Doctor found himself travelling with a young human waitress called Ace.

If the character of Mel had been something of a return to the archetypal screamer so prevalent during the sixties, Ace proved to be the complete opposite. From the very beginning, she was devised by script editor Andrew Cartmel and John Nathan-Turner as a strong female character who rarely shied away from the action, however

Nicola Bryant pictured in 1983.

'People seem to think I eat, sleep and drink dancing, and that I get up bouncing.'

Bonnie Langford

Bonnie Langford visits Mel's home town.

THE TARDIS LOG

Name: Melanie (Mel) Bush.

Occupation: Computer programmer.

Origin: Earth, England, 1980s.

Likes: Keeping fit, dancing, singing, smiling and being jolly.

Dislikes: Unfit people who don't like singing, dancing and being jolly.

Joined the Doctor because: Unknown. He must have been desperate for company.

Left the Doctor because: She fancied travelling with Sabalom Glitz.

Companion most likely to: Open a gym.

General Description: The kind of bubbly personality that can really get on your nerves.

Scream Factor: ★★★★★ And that was the audience.

Top right: Sophie Aldred in the 1993 West End musical comedy, Lust.

Ace dons forties clothes for an adventure in wartime Britain. The Curse of Fenric.

frightening it might be.

The character was initially called Alf, and on 26 January 1987, Cartmel and Nathan-Turner formulated the following description:

Alf is a teenage London girl who used to work on the till in a supermarket, until she was swept away from Earth by a time storm. The Doctor finds her in a distant galaxy… working on the till in a supermarket. Fed up with her routine job, determined to see the sights of the universe, Alf pours a drink into her talking till, quits and joins the Doctor on his adventures in the TARDIS.

Alf is uneducated but sharp, nobody's fool. She has a sense of wonder about their travels through time and space. She is smart and tough but protective of the Doctor. Can also be stroppy and sullen. She approaches her cosmic adventuring with a down to earth pragmatism and a somewhat off beat sense of humour.

Cartmel and Nathan-Turner were unsure as to when the character would actually be introduced. There was uncertainty as to whether Bonnie Langford was staying on as Mel and also as to the order of transmission of the final two stories. Therefore, Cartmel identified a couple of characters within the scripts in progress as potential companions.

The first of these was a character called Rachel, or Ray, who appeared in Malcolm Kohll's *Delta and the Bannermen*. Ray could have been adapted to the 'streetwise' definition of Alf, and was described as having 'innocence and openness about her' in the casting notes. She also had to be able to ride a motor-scooter.

The script that was ultimately to introduce the new companion, *Dragonfire*, was commissioned from writer Ian Briggs as a storyline on 9 March 1987. Along the way, the character's name was amended to Ace.

In the casting notes for Ace, the character was described as 'a very streetwise, athletic, snappy 18-year-old girl from Perivale. She's bright and sparky, is good at chemistry and has a ready wit. Can turn her hand to anything and shows no fear. Is used to looking after herself'. At this point, she was just a character in Briggs's script, but when Langford ultimately decided to bow out in *Dragonfire*, Nathan-Turner and Cartmel decided to keep Ace on, and requested Briggs to provide both a revised ending for the story to accommodate this and to sign an affidavit stating that Ace was henceforth the copyright property of the BBC.

The actress who ended up playing Ace, Sophie Aldred, had initially thought she was auditioning for the role of Ray. 'My agent called me and said that she'd got me an audition for three episodes of *Doctor Who*,' recalled Sophie. 'They were apparently looking for somebody who looked younger than they actually were and who could ride a motorbike. So I went off down to London from Manchester, never

Director Chris Clough discusses a scene with Sophie Aldred and Sylvester McCoy. Silver Nemesis.

THE TARDIS LOG

Name: Dorothy (nicknamed 'Ace').

Occupation: Waitress.

Origin:, Earth, England (Perivale), 1980s.

Likes: Explosives (Nitro-9), badges, saying 'Ace!' a lot.

Dislikes: Clowns, Perivale, her Mum.

Joined the Doctor because: She was bored of being a waitress on Iceworld and wanted to blow things up.

Left the Doctor because: She was still with the Doctor at the end of his television adventures.

General Description: A street-wise tomboy with a kind heart.

Companion most likely to: Get a *Blue Peter* badge for making bombs out of toilet rolls and sticky-back plastic.

Scream Factor: Ace isn't scared of anything, and even if she were she wouldn't scream.

having auditioned for telly before, met Chris Clough, the director, and we had this rather serious conversation about the state of children's theatre in Britain and I read what I later realised was one of Ace's speeches from *Dragonfire* but with 'Ace' scrubbed out and 'Ray' written in. Then a couple of weeks later, I heard that the producer wanted to meet me. So I went and met John Nathan-Turner and I had to read the same speech again to him. I didn't hear anything for ages until I was contacted by my agent and she told me that I'd got a part in three episodes and also that there was a faint possibility that I might be carrying on as the next new companion. I was really shocked because I'd never even been in front of a television camera!'

Like other actresses before her, Sophie found that she was not given much to go on to create the character. 'Basically I went into rehearsals and that was it. I found it quite difficult at first because having been used to the theatre, I was used to knowing more about the character. In fact, I became quite worried because I was playing this sixteen-year-old and I was 25 at the time so I wondered if I should play it down a bit more in age. I also wondered if she should have more of a Cockney accent, as that was what Ian had scripted. So in the end I went to the director and I told him my worries and he said, "No, what you're doing is fine, carry on," which was not what I wanted to hear in a way. I wanted to have some direction but in fact it turned out fine. I didn't actually base my performance on anyone I knew, although Ian had based the character on several kids that he worked with at Questor's Youth Theatre.'

Ace was already carrying a great deal of emotional baggage when the Doctor and Mel first encountered her in a bar on the ice planet of Svartos. Ace – who hated her real name of Dorothy – had often been in trouble with authority figures and had an extremely strained relationship with her parents. Her love of high explosives had caused her to be swept across the galaxy in a time storm to the ice planet.

The Doctor and Ace quickly established a rapport, assuming a

Sophie Aldred appears at her first press call with Sylvester McCoy.

ACE

Name: 'Ace' is her nickname. She's ashamed of her real name, and only told Mel in a moment of intimacy. (I feel that she would only ever tell another girl; not a man or a boy – probably not even the Doctor.) Her real name is Dorothy. I didn't specify a surname; it can be either the surname of Dorothy in *The Wizard of Oz*, or something that works in the context of the story it appears in – or, more likely, she'll just avoid the question and keep it secret.

Age: At the point of her appearance in *Dragonfire*, she was meant to be sixteen years and eleven months. In fact, she's based on three girls I know, all of whom are fourteen, so she has the personality and maturity of a young (rather than middling) teenager.

Home: She comes from Perivale, which she regards as the pits of London. As far as she's concerned, the only good thing about Perivale is that it has two tube stations! (One of the girls she's based on actually said this while watching a recording.)

Family: She doesn't have any brothers or sisters. If she did, she'd have mentioned them in her intimate speech to Mel. Besides, she's too much of a loner inside. She didn't get on with her parents, and she gets angry simply at the mention of them. Sometimes she refuses to accept that she even has any parents; at other times she wants to believe that her 'real' parents – the kind, loving ones – are somewhere else, maybe on another planet. But however bad a picture she paints of them, the truth is that her parents are an ordinary middle-class couple who always kept their feelings hidden, and didn't know how to cope with their tearaway daughter.

School: She enjoyed chemistry and was taking it at A-Level – although she would probably have failed because she isn't the academic type. She got suspended from school when she blew up the art room.

History: While she was at school she also had a boring evening job working in a fast-food cafeteria. She also used to do experiments with explosives in her bedroom, and it was an accident with one of these that triggered a time storm and carried her to Iceworld – where she again found work as a waitress.

Speech: She uses phrases typical of London teenagers: 'Wicked!', 'Well worth!', 'Naff!' and of course 'Ace!' I don't care if, technically, she left Perivale in early 1987, and so ought still to be using the phrases of that period; the more current and realistic her speech, the better. She coins nicknames for everybody, such as 'doughnut' for Mel, and 'bilgebag' for Glitz. And even though it irritates the Doctor, she can't help calling him 'Professor'. The only time she reverts to using real names is when she's frightened, as when Kane was holding her hostage in *Dragonfire*.

Personality: Typical teenager really. Bright and full of life one moment; spiky and argumentative the next. Even though she likes the Doctor, she's bound to come over all moody and complaining with him from time to time. A particular characteristic is her heightened sense of excitement, which sometimes overrides her sense of danger: her immediate reaction on first seeing the creature in *Dragonfire* was to yell with delight, and only later did she think to run like hell!

**From the Script writer's guide.
October 1987**

Right: the Doctor and Ace in The Curse of Fenric.

teacher and student relationship as Ace began to grow from an awkward teenager into a more mature adult. Sophie puts this down to getting on well with Sylvester McCoy. 'I hit it off with Sylvester,' she explained. 'And I think that was the most important thing really about the whole of our working relationship – the fact that we did have some chemistry there.'

Before the scripts were complete for the 25th season, Andrew Cartmel arranged for Sophie to meet some of the writers to give them an idea of what she and her character were like and to enable them to draw on that. 'I'd also been doing *Corners* back to back with *Doctor Who*,' adds Sophie. 'And so by the time *Remembrance of the Daleks* came along, I was so much more confident with the medium of television anyway. I can't remember feeling at all worried about it and I never really considered my characterisation. It was something that seemed to come quite naturally.'

Writers subsequently commissioned by Cartmel to work on the series responded to his and Sylvester McCoy's desire to bring some darkness into the Doctor, especially in the Gothic *Ghost Light* and *The Curse of Fenric*, in which the Doctor confronted an old – but so far unseen in the series – adversary, and discovered that Fenric had been manipulating Ace all along and had caused the time storm which brought her into contact with him in the first place. By the time Ace and the Doctor strolled off into the sunset at the end of the last televised story to date, *Survival*, Ace was a character much more at peace with herself than she had been at the start of their travels. In fact, Ace underwent a greater process of on-screen development than any other *Doctor Who* companion in the previous 26 years of the programme.

At the time, none of the cast really knew that *Survival* was to be the last televised story, especially as it was not the last one to be recorded. 'We just went and did *Survival* then came back, had a breather, and went straight into a read-through for *Ghost Light*,' explained Sophie. 'Looking back on it now, I had a really, really fantastic time – most of the time – working on it because it was such a good atmosphere. My working relationship with Sylvester was just brilliant, all the technical crews that we worked with were superb… It really was like halcyon days. So I would say that it was incredibly enjoyable and a brilliant learning experience – wicked, in fact.'

With the series ending on television in 1989 – apart from the brief appearance of Ace and the seventh Doctor in *Dimensions in Time* in 1993 – the Doctor and Ace's adventures transferred to a different medium when in 1989 Virgin Publishing began to release a series of connected novels following their adventures after the conclusion of *Survival*. This range of books heralded a new phase for the character of Ace and for *Doctor Who* itself.

'What I didn't realise at the time, because I was very inexperienced in television and it was my first real television job, was how lucky I was to have that enormous experience in such a short time.'

Sophie Aldred

FUTURE MATTERS: A NOVEL SOLUTION

The Doctor's granddaughter Susan (Roberta Tovey), from the film Dr. Who and the Daleks.

Right: Jill Curzon took the role of the Doctor's niece Louise in the second film, Daleks' Invasion Earth 2150 AD. This shot is not from the film.

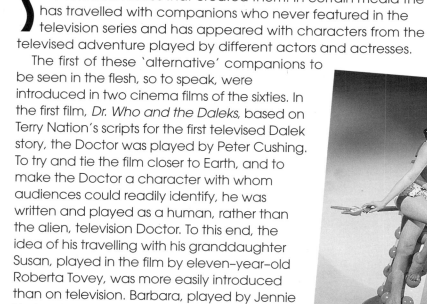

Ian (Roy Castle), Dr Who (Peter Cushing), Barbara (Jennie Linden) and Susan (Roberta Tovey) are held prisoner by the Daleks. Dr. Who and the Daleks.

everal of the Doctor's companions have appeared in works outside the television series that created them. In certain media the Doctor has travelled with companions who never featured in the television series and has appeared with characters from the televised adventure played by different actors and actresses.

The first of these 'alternative' companions to be seen in the flesh, so to speak, were introduced in two cinema films of the sixties. In the first film, *Dr. Who and the Daleks*, based on Terry Nation's scripts for the first televised Dalek story, the Doctor was played by Peter Cushing. To try and tie the film closer to Earth, and to make the Doctor a character with whom audiences could readily identify, he was written and played as a human, rather than the alien, television Doctor. To this end, the idea of his travelling with his granddaughter Susan, played in the film by eleven-year-old Roberta Tovey, was more easily introduced than on television. Barbara, played by Jennie Linden, became the Doctor's other granddaughter and Ian, brought to life by Roy Castle in his second film role, was her bumbling boyfriend.

'I was a fan of the television series,' remembered Tovey, speaking in 1993, 'but I didn't try to copy Carole Ann Ford's Susan. We stamped our own identities on it.' Tovey was chosen for the part after auditioning for the film's director, Gordon Flemyng, with other children from the Corona Stage School. She was called for a film test down at Shepperton Studios and by the time she returned home from the test, she had been offered the part.

'The characters have been changed to a certain extent,' said Jennie Linden when interviewed at the time. 'Barbara is now about 20 – that's the part I play. My boyfriend is Roy Castle and Peter Cushing is Dr. Who.'

Roy Castle commented in another period interview: 'In this one I'm not playing it for laughs, although I've never tackled anything really serious and have always been light-hearted in my performances.'

In the second film, the characters veered wildly from those established on television. In *Daleks Invasion Earth 2150 AD*, again based on a television story (*The Dalek Invasion of Earth*), the Doctor was again played by Cushing, with Roberta Tovey reprising her role as his granddaughter. Jill Curzon was brought in to play Louise, the Doctor's niece, and to play the young male lead, comedy actor Bernard Cribbins was cast as Tom, a policeman who, witnessing a robbery, finds himself in the TARDIS after mistaking it for a real police call box.

The television companions have also appeared in many other stories and productions over the years. Susan Foreman turned up in an episode of the 1994 radio series *Whatever Happened To...* when the character was voiced by Jane Asher. The Brigadier and Sarah Jane Smith both appeared in the radio productions *The Paradise of Death* and *The Ghosts of N–Space*, as well as *Dimensions in Time* on television and the *Downtime* video project. Sarah appeared with the Doctor, played by Tom Baker, in an episode of the *Exploration Earth* radio series in 1974, as well as in an audio adventure called *Doctor Who and the Pescatons*. Sergeant Benton went on to appear in Reeltime Pictures' video drama *Wartime* and, together with Mike Yates and the voice of the Brigadier, in the play *Recall UNIT*. Harry Sullivan and Turlough turned up in original novels: *Harry Sullivan's War* written by Ian Marter and *Turlough and the Earthlink Dilemma* written by Tony Attwood. Peri was teamed with the sixth Doctor for a radio drama called *Slipback* which was transmitted during the programme's hiatus in 1985.

Many of the companions have also appeared in the various *Doctor Who* comic strips and text stories published over the years, including a series of novels published by Virgin Publishing bearing the overall title of *The Missing Adventures*, and a series of short-story collections from the same publisher with the generic title of *Decalog*.

When *Doctor Who* transferred to the stage in 1974, in a play written by Terrance Dicks and called *Doctor Who and the Daleks in Seven Keys to Doomsday*, the Doctor, played by Trevor Martin, was joined by two young helpers who apparently went up onto the stage from the audience to help him as he lay regenerating on the stage floor at the start of each performance. These two good Samaritans were Jenny and Jimmy, played by Wendy Padbury and James Mathews. The idea of them joining the action from the audience was felt to be an effective way of making the other children feel that, had they only stepped in to help the Doctor at the start, then they too could have been with him as he battled with the Daleks.

The next *Doctor Who* stage play was again written by Terrance Dicks and went under the title *The Ultimate Adventure*. In this 1989 offering, the Doctor was played by Jon Pertwee for the first part of the show's tour and then by Colin Baker, with actor David Banks stepping in for one performance when Pertwee fell ill. At the start of the adventure, the Doctor was travelling with a young

Crystal (Rebecca Thornhill), the Doctor (Colin Baker) and Jason (Graeme Smith) in The Ultimate Adventure *stage play.*

The Doctor's first cartoon-strip companions John and Gillian who appeared in TV Comic.

man from revolutionary France named Jason (Graeme Smith). Along the way, they picked up nightclub singer Crystal (Rebecca Thornhill) and Zog (Stephanie Colburn), an alien dog-like creature. This unlikely band of travellers helped defeat an invasion by the Cybermen, the Daleks and a band of mercenaries led by the dastardly Karl, brought to life by David Banks who had also played the Cyberleader in *Doctor Who* on television.

Companions to have appeared in other media include John and Gillian,

two young children who were introduced in the first ever *Doctor Who* comic strip which appeared in *TV Comic* issue 674 (November 1964). In the story entitled *The Klepton Parasites*, they were looking for their grandfather who apparently lived at 'number 16' in an unnamed road. 'Number 16' was just a yard, however, and in it stood the TARDIS. Their grandfather – who was here called Doctor Who – was inside and when John activated the controls out of curiosity, they were all plunged headlong into an adventure against the dreaded Kleptons.

In the pages of *Doctor Who Weekly* (and later *Doctor Who Monthly* and *Doctor Who Magazine*) we were introduced to Sharon in *The Star Beast* (issue 19, published February 1980). A young girl from the fictional town of Blackcastle, she travelled with the Doctor for several issues, growing up into a young lady with a penchant for tight-fitting cat–suits. Later came Frobisher, the shape–changing whifferdill who normally appeared as a penguin. He arrived in a strip called *The Shape Shifter* (issue 88, May 1984). Other strips featured one-off companions, or the characters travelled for only a few stories.

Following the end of *Doctor Who* on television in 1989, the Doctor and Ace continued their adventures in a series of novels from Virgin Publishing. The novels, collectively called *The New Adventures* were, as the title suggested, new stories. Written by fans of the series, professionals

Right: Visual effects designer Mike Tucker helps Sophie Aldred into a rubber suit made to resemble Ace's combat outfit, worn by the character in the New Adventures novels, and as pictured by artist Tony Masero for the cover of First Frontier *(below). The costume was re-created especially for a set of photographs which appear in Sophie Aldred and Mike Tucker's behind-the-scenes book entitled* Ace!

who had worked on it and aspiring new writers, the range of material the books featured was nothing short of breathtaking.

In the initial writers' guidelines for the novels, series editor Peter Darvill-Evans stated his intent that Ace should have grown up from the character we last saw on television. 'She is still impetuous, insightful, impatient with authority and scathing of bullshit,' he wrote, 'full of energy and vehemently anti-racist; but she is also clever, resourceful and daring, and she has learned a lot in her travels with the Doctor.'

Darvill-Evans went on to discuss other aspects of Ace's character and ended with the comment that Ian Briggs, the creator of Ace in the television story *Dragonfire*, who had just completed the novelisation of his story *The Curse of Fenric*, had stressed that 'the crucial event in *Fenric* is Ace's growing up. She becomes, at least in some ways, a match for the Doctor.'

As the range progressed, we started to find out more about Ace's background, to a greater degree than had ever been revealed on television. In Paul Cornell's 1991 novel *Timewyrm: Revelation*, we learned of Ace's childhood and following this, the character became far more intricate and complex.

Ultimately Ace decided to stop travelling with the Time Lord (in Paul Cornell's 1992 book *Love and War*) but she was back in 1993 in Peter Darvill-Evans's own *Deceit*. She was now three years older, and had spent time with a crack troop of Spacefleet Auxiliaries, hunting and destroying Daleks across the universe. The new Ace was harder, tougher and altogether more uncompromising than her previous self. Gone were the occasional tantrums and trust in the Doctor, and in came mistrust and a constant feeling that the Doctor wasn't telling the whole story.

'These days she thinks before she speaks,' stated Virgin's writer's guide, 'and she's learned to control her anger. But in a way these changes only make her even more dangerous. Don't get mad, get even – that's her motto.'

Eventually it was time for Ace to move on again, and in Kate Orman's 1995 novel *Set Piece* she ended up living in nineteenth-century France, thus

Artist Lee Sullivan was asked by Virgin Publishing and Marvel Comics to produce a set of concept sketches for the character of Benny to aid future cover artists and writers with her appearance.

Lee Sullivan's design sketches for the cover of Paul Cornell's novel Love and War, *which introduced the character of Bernice Summerfield.*

linking in with a point of continuity present in Ian Briggs's 1990 novelisation of *The Curse of Fenric,* but not present in the actual televised adventure.

As companions leave in *The New Adventures,* so new companions are introduced, and in *Love and War,* Cornell brought in a character to replace Ace.

This was Professor Bernice Summerfield, otherwise known as Benny. She was an archaeologist from Earth's future who was living and working on a planet called Heaven when the Doctor and Ace arrived there. In many respects, she was a normal, human woman with an insatiable curiosity about all things, but particularly in the matter of her father, long missing, and long regarded as a traitor. She went out into the universe partly to find him.

'Benny came into *Love And War* as a deliberate companion audition, a result of the same process that produced Kadiatu (the Brigadier's granddaughter, a character who first appeared in Ben Aaronovitch's novel *Transit,* published immediately after *Love and War*),' explained Paul Cornell. 'I wanted to create a companion who was more mature than usual (Benny is 32), and also one who was, as much as possible, a bit more like a real woman. I mean that, rather than being Rambo with ovaries, this is somebody who thinks that the whole macho thing is a bit silly and that the most powerful group of people in the world are four women with a jug of sangria between them.'

Benny was the one who considered what was happening to the little person as a result of the Doctor's big plans. She wasn't fond of big things, like the military (having narrowly avoided serving in it) or big organisations, and liked to poke fun at them through her sarcasm and wit.

Through successive adventures, Benny became as well known and identifiable to the reader as Ace, which was impressive as with Ace, there was the advantage of having seen an actress perform the role on television. With Benny there was no such luxury, although Paul Cornell once commented that he based her on the actress Emma Thompson. He also said: 'She's me in a frock!'

Another addition to the TARDIS crew came when Paul Cornell introduced a cat, Wolsey, on board in his 1995 novel *Human Nature.* Wolsey is a perfectly ordinary, tabby tom-cat from Earth, which the Doctor takes on board the TARDIS when his previous owner can't keep him.

Having made the decision to write Ace out of the novels, Virgin was keen to see some new companions introduced to take her place. 'It all started at a party held by Virgin for all their authors in 1993,' explained Andy Lane, the author who created the new characters. 'There was a lot of discussion between the various authors who had gathered together as to whether there should be any new companions and if so, who they should be. I was pushing very hard for a change in the way the people in the TARDIS related to each other. What I wanted was an elderly companion, someone who looked a lot older than the Doctor and who could treat the Doctor as a son, much to the Doctor's disgust. I proposed a 70-year-old tramp character called Old Tom, whose brain was half fried from various experiences in his past and an awful lot of drink, but who had some deep, dark, terrible secret. In fact, the secret that I hadn't actually told Virgin was that he was Bernice's dad.

'Virgin had sort of agreed to this, and I got about 20,000 words into *Original Sin*, the novel that was to introduce the new character, and he just wasn't working. Old Tom was basically just not a very good companion. I was getting more and more depressed when writing the book because I realised that he wasn't working and was going to have to admit that I had been wrong. Then I telephoned Rebecca, the editor at Virgin, and was about to explain the problem when she said something like: "Before you do, can I tell you something? We don't like Old Tom." Then she said, "But don't worry. We like these two Adjudicator characters you've got. We think they're brilliant."

Following Virgin Publishing's lead, Marvel's Doctor Who Magazine *printed a cartoon-strip featuring the New Adventures-style Ace, Benny and the Doctor. The story was called* Final Genesis *and was drawn by Colin Andrew.*

'The Adjudicators had started as minor characters but I had grown to like them more and more as I was writing the book. I really loved writing the dialogue for them: it was snappy and they got all the funny lines, so I went back and rewrote the first 20,000 words and got rid of the tramp character – I made him into an alien – and played off the other two as being the companions and it all fell beautifully into place.'

Published in 1995, *Original Sin* introduced the Adjudicators from the Earth Empire era (around the 30th century). They were Roslyn Forrester, older, female, worldly (or should that be universe-ly) wise and cynically wearied by all she surveys, and her rookie partner Chris Cwej, (pronounced Kwedge), a young, enthusiastic and infuriatingly naïve young man, who always saw the good in everyone and everything.

Forrester couldn't shoot straight and came from a powerful, rich, pure-bred family which was a part of the Earth Empire's aristocracy. She could have become the Baroness of Io when her father died but renounced the title as she was rebelling against the aristocratic lifestyle. Cwej, on the other hand, came from a poor but very large and happy family. All his male ancestors were Adjudicators and so it seemed natural that he would follow the same path.

These two enjoyed sparring verbally with each other and provided a perfect foil for the Doctor. As Paul Cornell had visualised Bernice, so Lane had a basis for his characters: 'As I was writing them I found them to be a strange mix between Han Solo and the Wookie Chewbacca from the *Star Wars* films, and also characters from the television series *NYPD Blue*. This made it a lot easier to write distinctive dialogue for two very different characters.'

After 30-plus companions have come and gone, the Doctor's adventures continue. Whether they will only be on paper or once again on our television screens only the future knows, but as long as the Doctor keeps his most faithful companions – the viewers and fans – then his journeys will never end.

INDEX OF COMPANIONS

The following index is in order of the name that the Doctor's companions are best known by, with their full name following in brackets.

ACE

ADRIC

BARBARA

BEN

BENTON

BRIGADIER

DODO

HARRY

Name: Ace (Dorothy)
Played by: **Sophie Aldred**
Years: **1987–9**
Doctor: **Sylvester McCoy (7)**

Sophie Aldred was born in 1962 and brought up in Blackheath, southeast London. After leaving school, she attended Manchester University, where she took a degree in drama. After University she sang in working men's clubs to obtain her Equity card, then worked in children's theatre, appeared in a fringe show, *Underground Man*, at a pub theatre in London to get an agent, followed by more children's theatre. She was appearing in *Fiddler on the Roof* with Topol in Manchester when she landed the part of Ace. At the same time as appearing in *Doctor Who*, she presented a series for young children called *Corners* and later *Melvin and Maureen's Music–a–grams*, which combined her acting and music skills. She has appeared in a number of theatre productions including a tour of *Daisy Pulls it Off* in which she played the lead; she also played Marjorie Pinchwife in the 1993 West End production of *Lust*, a version of *The Country Wife*. In 1995 she worked for the Children's Channel on satellite and also *Love Call Live* for Anglia television with David 'Kid' Jensen.

Name: Adric
Played by: **Matthew Waterhouse**
Years: **1980–2**
Doctor: **Tom Baker (4)/ Peter Davison (5)**

Born in 1962, the son of a company solicitor, Matthew Waterhouse joined the BBC working in the news and information department. His first acting role was as a public schoolboy in *To Serve Them All My Days* (1980) and he had not even started working on that programme before he auditioned for and got the role of Adric in *Doctor Who*. Since leaving the show, Waterhouse has worked in the theatre, appearing as Puck in *A Midsummer Night's Dream*, as Peter in *Peter Pan* and as Edmund in *The Lion, the Witch and the Wardrobe*. He also appeared in a one–man show, *The Adventures of Huckleberry Finn*, which he adapted from Mark Twain's novel.

Name: Barbara Wright
Played by: **Jacqueline Hill**
Years: **1963–5**
Doctor: **William Hartnell (1)**

Jacqueline Hill was born on 17 December 1929. She set her heart on an acting career at an early age and managed to secure herself a much-prized scholarship to attend the Royal Academy of Dramatic Art (RADA). After graduating, her first role came in a production of *The Shrink*, directed by Sam Wanamaker. This small part led to an appearance in the 1954 television production of *Three Empty Rooms*. Further theatre and television work followed, including *Requiem for a Heavyweight* written by Rod Serling, creator of *The Twilight Zone* and directed by her husband Alvin Rakoff. She also appeared in a number of films including *The Blue Parrot* (1953) and *The Comedy Man* (1963). After leaving her role as Barbara in *Doctor Who*, she gave up acting to raise her family, resuming her career again in the late seventies with roles in television including *Romeo and Juliet* (1978) and *Tales of the Unexpected* as well as returning to *Doctor Who* in 1980 to play the high priestess Lexa in the fourth Doctor story *Meglos*. Jacqueline Hill died on 18 February 1993 after succumbing to a long illness which had curtailed her career in later years.

Name: Ben Jackson
Played by: **Michael Craze**
Years: **1966–7**
Doctor: **William Hartnell (1)/ Patrick Troughton (2)**

Michael Craze was born in Cornwall on 29 November 1942. He fell into the world of acting by chance, when he took part in Boy Scout gang shows and discovered he had a perfect boy soprano voice. This led to parts in productions of *The King and I* and *Plain and Fancy* at Drury Lane. After leaving school, he performed in repertory theatre and was later pushed into television by his agent. After appearing in programmes like *Armchair Theatre: The Pillars of Midnight* (1958) and *Target Luna* (1960), he was offered the role of Ben in *Doctor Who*. He appeared in *Gideon's Way: Boy with a Gun* (1966) and *No Hiding Place: A Bottle Full of Scorpions* (1966). In the seventies and eighties, he managed a number of public houses while continuing to take the occasional acting part. In 1994, he appeared in the television play *The Healer* as well as doing several days' work on Kenneth Branagh's 1994 movie adaptation of *Mary Shelley's Frankenstein*.

Name: Benton, Sergeant
Played by: **John Levene**
Years: **1968–75**

Doctor: **Patrick Troughton (2)/ Jon Pertwee (3)/Tom Baker (4)**

John Levene was born John Woods in 1941 in Salisbury. He left home at 21 and went to London, where he ended up working in a men's clothing store in Regent Street. He decided to become an actor when American Telly Savalas came into the store and suggested that he could offer John a part as an extra in a film in which he was involved. Levene discovered that he couldn't take the part as he didn't have the required Equity card. He therefore signed on at an agency which supplied walk-on actors and his first job was in *Adam Adamant Lives!*. He also appeared in *Z Cars* and several other television shows, including *Doctor Who*, where he appeared as a Cyberman in *The Moonbase* (1967) and a Yeti in *The Web of Fear* (1968) and *The War Games* (1969). It was director Douglas Camfield who offered Levene the part of Benton in *The Invasion* (1968). The character went on to become one of the regular team of UNIT personnel from the season-seven story *The Ambassadors of Death* up until *The Android Invasion* in 1975. Other television included *Callan* (1970) and *The Adventurer* (1972); he also appeared in the film *Go For a Take* (1972). In 1977, Levene gave up acting and set up his own audio-visuals company which specialised in conference presentations. More recently, he has worked as a compère and entertainer on cruise liners and has now emigrated to the USA where he has returned to acting, continuing his work as an entertainer under the name John Anthony Blake. In 1988, he reprised his role as Benton in the direct-to-video drama *Wartime*.

Name: Brigadier Alistair Gordon Lethbridge–Stewart
Played by: **Nicholas Courtney**
Years: **1968–89**
Doctor: **All but Colin Baker**

Nicholas Courtney's father was a diplomat serving in Egypt where Courtney was born in 1931. He spent several years in Kenya and France while growing up and at the age of eighteen, found himself called up for National Service. Following the end of his eighteen-month duty, Courtney did several temporary jobs until he auditioned for and was accepted by the Webber Douglas drama school. He left after two years and worked in repertory at Northampton before moving to London in 196. He started in television with roles in *Sword of Honour*, *Watch the Birdies* (1966) and other productions. In 1965 he was cast by

director Douglas Camfield to appear in the twelve-part *Doctor Who* story *The Daleks' Master Plan*. Then, in 1967, he was again cast by Camfield to play Colonel Lethbridge-Stewart in *The Web of Fear*. He played the character off and on for the next 23 years. In between appearances in *Doctor Who*, Courtney appeared in stage productions of *The Dame of Sark*, *Donkey's Years*, *The Rocky Horror Show* and *The Mousetrap* as well as on television, in *Then Churchill Said To Me* (1980), *Minder* (1984), *Juliet Bravo*, *All Creatures Great and Small* and *Sink or Swim*. His film work includes *To Catch A King* (1984) and the television film *Jenny's War* (1984). In 1995 he appeared, again playing the Brigadier, in the direct-to-video drama *Downtime*.

Name: Dodo (Dorothea Chaplet)
Played by: **Jackie Lane**
Years: **1966**
Doctor: **William Hartnell (1)**

Jacqueline Joyce Lane was born on 10 July 1947 in Manchester, the daughter of John and Ena. After being educated at Whalley Range High school, she worked at the Manchester Library Theatre for two years. In 1962 she came to London and gained a small part in a BBC television play as well as appearing in *Z Cars* and *The Reluctant Debutante* at the Golders Green Hippodrome. In 1963 she appeared on the BBC's *Monitor* programme and had a small part in the soap opera *Compact*; she was also considered for the part of the Doctor's granddaughter, Susan. Her film appearances include *Men of Sherwood Forest*, *The Gamma People* (1956), *Tickle Me* (1965), *The Sword of Ali Baba*, *Incident at Phantom Hill* (1966) and *Land Raiders* (1970). In 1966 she accepted an offer from John Wiles to play teenager Dorothea Chaplet. After *Doctor Who* she made one brief appearance in *Pinocchio* at Bromley Rep before giving up acting and going to work as a secretary in the Australian embassy in Paris. She returned to England some time later and ran an antiques business for around six years, then joined London Management, a theatrical management company, moving on to run a specialist voice-over department for the agency.

Name: Harry Sullivan
Played by: **Ian Marter**
Years: **1974–5**
Doctor: **Tom Baker (4)**

Ian Marter began his acting career after leaving university in 1969 when he entered the Bristol Old Vic as an acting stage manager. His first professional part was as a Russian soldier in *The Hostage*. It was around 1973 that he started looking for television roles and one of the first parts he played was John Andrews in the 1973 *Doctor Who* story *Carnival of Monsters*. Marter then returned to the theatre before being offered the part of Harry Sullivan in 1974. In 1976 Marter, along with Tom Baker and James Hill, developed the idea for a *Doctor Who* feature film called *Doctor Who meets Scratchman*. Marter also proved himself a talented writer, novelising several *Doctor Who* stories for the Target range, as well as completing a full length original novel, *Harry Sullivan's War*. Marter novelised several films, including *Baby* and *Splash*, written under the pen name of Ian Don, and *My Science Project* under his own name. He was partway through the novelisation of the William Hartnell *Doctor Who* story *The Rescue* when he died suddenly in his London home on 30 October 1986. The novel was subsequently completed by Nigel Robinson, the editor of the range of books at the time. Marter's last work in front of the cameras was for Reeltime Pictures, who had recorded a lengthy interview/drama with him for their *Myth Makers* interview series six weeks previously.

Name: **Ian Chesterton**
Played by: **William Russell**
Years: **1963–5**
Doctor: **William Hartnell (1)**

Russell William Enoch became interested in acting at school and made his first stage appearance at the age of eight as the Mock Turtle in a school production of *Alice in Wonderland*. He was involved in organising entertainment during his National Service in the Royal Air Force and then, after completing his university education, went into repertory and worked for Bristol Old Vic. He appeared in Alec Guinness's *Hamlet* in London's West End and won a number of film roles, including *They Who Dare* (1954) and *The Man Who Never Was* (1956). He began acting under the name William Russell when he appeared in the film *One Good Turn* (1954) with Norman Wisdom. His first television work was the title role in *Young Renny* (1954), a play by Canadian authoress Mazo de la Roche. Other leading roles followed including *St. Ives* in 1955, *The Adventures of Sir Lancelot* for Sapphire Films, *David Copperfield* (1956) and *Nicholas Nickleby* (1957) for the BBC. He was then cast as Ian Chesterton in *Doctor Who*. He later continued his acting career in the theatre, joining the Old Vic, the Royal Shakespeare Company and the National Theatre. In the late eighties he appeared as a regular character in *Coronation Street*. He also held a senior post in the actors' union, Equity for a time. In the early eighties he toured South America, Brazil, Argentina, Chile, Europe, Ireland, Sweden and Romania. He married actress Balbina in 1953 and has three children.

Name: **Jamie (James Robert McCrimmon)**
Played by: **Frazer Hines**
Years: **1966–9**
Doctor: **Patrick Troughton (2)**

Frazer Hines was born on 22 September 1944 in Horsforth, Yorkshire. After studying acting at the Corona Academy, he made his professional debut at the age of eight. He appeared in Charlie Chaplin's *A King in New York* (1957) when he was thirteen and by the age of fifteen, he had appeared in six films. In 1960 he appeared in the eight-part cinema serial *The Young Jacobites*. His first major television role was in *The Silver Sword* (1957–8) followed by appearances in *Emergency Ward Ten* (1963) and *Coronation Street* (1965). After his three years as Jamie, in *Doctor Who* he eventually landed the role of Joe Sugden in the long-running soap opera *Emmerdale Farm*. In the eighties, Frazer returned twice to the role of Jamie in *The Five Doctors* and *The Two Doctors*, while continuing to appear in other television shows. In 1994, he left *Emmerdale* – as the show had been retitled in the eighties. He now lives with his second wife Liz Hobbs and together they pursue their love of racing horses, managing their own stud farm. He still acts, appearing on stage in *Not Now Darling* (1994) and making occasional guest appearances on television.

Name: **Jo Grant**
Played by: **Katy Manning**
Years: **1971–3**
Doctor: **Jon Pertwee (3)**

Katy Manning was born in 1948, the daughter of the late sports columnist J. L. Manning. At sixteen, she had a car accident which put her in hospital for a year, but two years later she went to America and was offered a five-year contract with MGM. Her father, however, insisted that she return to England and study acting. She trained at the Webber Douglas drama school for a year before joining a Wolverhampton repertory company. Her first job was in *Man at the Top* (1970) with Kenneth Haigh. Manning found that her height – only five feet – was a disadvantage in theatre and so she moved to television where it was not so much of a problem. She made several commercials for ITV before appearing in an episode of *Softly, Softly: Task Force*. She landed the part of Jo Grant in *Doctor Who* in 1970. After leaving *Doctor Who* she presented a crafts programme for the BBC called *Serendipity* (1973) and played Miss Damina in the film *Don't Just Lie There, Say Something* (1973). In the theatre she appeared with Derek Nimmo in *Why Not Stay for Breakfast* and with Lionel Blair and Colin Baker in *Odd Man In*. In 1975 she appeared on television in *Target: Big Elephant*. Manning married actor Raynor Burton in 1975, but the marriage lasted only five weeks. She had twins: a son, Jonathan, and a daughter, Georgina, by her boyfriend, actor Dean Harris, in 1978. Since 1982, she has been living and working in Australia.

Name: **K–9**
Voice by: **John Leeson/David Brierley**
Years: **1977–81**
Doctor: **Tom Baker (4)**

John Leeson: After leaving school John Leeson worked in a bookshop in Leicester before becoming a porter in the Leicester Royal Infirmary. It was while at the hospital that he joined the Leicester Dramatic Society and ultimately decided to apply to RADA for an audition. To his amazement he passed and was offered a place. On leaving RADA he found himself working in repertory and pantomimes including *Toad of Toad Hall* with Richard Goolden, in which he met his future wife. His first work on television was as a walk-on in a religious play, *The Wedding Feast*, for the BBC and he followed this with other appearances including *The Spanish Farm* (1968), *Dad's Army* and numerous situation comedies. He played the original Bungle the bear in the children's series *Rainbow* (1972), set questions for *Mastermind* and did a lot of freelance voice work for the BBC. The part of K-9's voice came about when he bumped into the director, with whom he had worked previously, in a pub. He was subsequently cast as the voice of K-9 and of the Nucleus in *The Invisible Enemy*. He was seen on-screen in *Doctor Who* when he took the part of Dugeen in *The Power of Kroll*. He stopped doing K-9's voice for a year as he felt he needed to get his face known, but in 1979, producer John Nathan-Turner asked if he would come back because David Brierley, who had provided the voice after Leeson had left, was unavailable for season eighteen. Since K-9 left *Doctor Who*, Leeson has continued to provide voice-over services for the BBC and many other companies. In 1995 he appeared in a direct-to-video *Doctor Who* spin-off drama called *Downtime*.

David Brierley: David Brierley was born in 1935 in Yorkshire. His many skills include being an expert sailor, a keen fell walker and a long-distance runner. He has worked in television on shows such as *Storytime*, *Blind Justice*, *Howard's Way*, *Cover her Face*, *The Tripods*, *Words and Pictures*, *Threads*, *Coronation Street*, *Juliet Bravo*, *The Law of the Land* and *Frankie Howerd Strikes Again*, as well as playing the voice of K-9 for season seventeen of *Doctor Who*. On radio he has appeared as Doctor Watson in *The Hound of the Baskervilles*, Brutus in *Julius Caesar*, Mercutio in *Romeo and Juliet* and Puck in *A Midsummer Night's Dream*. He has also enjoyed a theatre career which includes seasons at Richmond on the Green, Aldershot, Wimbledon, Ventnor and Northampton, with specific productions including *Sun of York* and *Sons of Oedipus*.

IAN

JAMIE

JO

K-9: K-9 (K to his friends) had wanted to break into acting ever since he was a pup. After several years of obedience school, K enrolled at RADA (Repertory for Artificial Dog Actors) but soon left to try his luck in Hollywood. For several years he worked as a stunt double for Lassie until he was spotted by George Lucas, who considered him for the part of R2D2 in *Star Wars* (1977). Lucas later decided to hire a dustbin instead. Dejected, K returned to England where his agent sent him to audition for a small part in *Doctor Who*. Producer Graham Williams was so pleased with K-9's performance that he offered him a regular part in the series. K-9 proved to be huge hit and was even given his own television special. The end was in sight when the script writers began to ask K to perform more of his own stunts: travelling on beaches, over muddy ground and going up and down stairs. K was unable to perform such complicated feats as his health had deteriorated since his Hollywood stunt-dog days. His co-stars reported that he became increasingly difficult to work with, and in a number of cases had to be written out of stories completely. Ultimately, K-9's contract was not renewed when it ran out midway through season eighteen. K-9 continues to make a living from his most famous role, occasionally appearing in educational programmes for children as well as infrequent guest appearances at conventions. He lives in Berkshire in semi-retirement.

K-9

Name: **Kamelion**
Voice by: **Gerald Flood**
Years: **1983–4**
Doctor: **Peter Davison (5)**

Gerald Flood was born in Portsmouth into a Naval family. He was a wireless operator during World War II then worked as a filing clerk until he landed a job with the Farnham Repertory Company. It was there that he met his future wife, Anne. He toured in rep, and appeared in productions like *Hamlet*, *Power and Glory* and *Charley's Aunt*. In 1960 he performed in *The Complaisant Lover* at the Globe

KAMELION

KATARINA

LEELA

LIZ

MEL

NYSSA

PERI

POLLY

Theatre and went on to appear in *The Formation Dancers*, *Children's Day* and *There's a Girl in my Soup*. In the 1960s he appeared in a science-fiction series called *Pathfinders In Space* (1960) and its sequels *Pathfinders to Mars* (1960–1)and *Pathfinders to Venus* (1961). Other television roles followed, including *The Ratcatchers* (1966–7), *A Sharp Intake of Breath*, *Third Time Lucky* and *Bleak House*. He also guested on shows like *Randall and Hopkirk, Deceased: A Disturbing Case* (1969), *Strange Report*, *Steptoe and Son: What Prejudice* (1970) and *Return of the Saint*. His films included *Black Beauty* (1946), *Patton* (1970), *Smokescreen* and *Frightmare* (1974). Gerald Flood died in April 1989.

Name: **Katarina**
Played by: **Adrienne Hill**
Years: **1965**
Doctor: **William Hartnell (1)**

Plymouth-born Adrienne Hill trained in acting at Bristol Old Vic, then spent some time with the Old Vic Company in London, followed by eight years' work in repertory theatre. Having been spotted by *Doctor Who* production assistant Viktors Ritelis while understudying for Maggie Smith in a play called *Mary, Mary*, she was invited to audition for the role of Princess Joanna in *The Crusade*. Although she did not win the part, director Douglas Camfield remembered her while casting for *The Daleks' Master Plan* and she was cast as Katarina in *The Myth Makers*. In the late sixties, she had continued success, particularly in radio, and landed a regular role in BBC Radio's *Waggoner's Walk*. She also appeared in *Compact* and *199 Park Lane* (1965) on television. She then moved abroad with her husband when his work took him to Holland and later to the USA. In the late seventies, after her marriage broke up, she returned to England and studied for a degree. During the eighties, she launched a new career as a drama teacher, while continuing to take occasional acting work.

Name: **Leela**
Played by: **Louise Jameson**
Years: **1977–8**
Doctor: **Tom Baker (4)**

Louise Jameson was born in 1951 in Wanstead, the daughter of an insurance broker. On leaving school, in 1966, she trained briefly as a secretary before auditioning for and joining RADA at the age of 17, where she trained from 1969 to 1971. Since leaving RADA, Jameson has rarely been out of work. She has appeared extensively in the theatre, working for the Royal Shakespeare Company on several occasions and touring both England and America. On television she first

appeared in *Cider with Rosie* and *Tom Brown's Schooldays* in 1971; other roles included *Z Cars* (1972), *Emmerdale Farm* (1973) and *Play For Today: The Peddler* (1976). She auditioned for and got the part of the savage Leela in *Doctor Who* in 1976. After leaving the programme in 1978, she went straight to Bristol Old Vic to play Portia in *The Merchant of Venice*. Other stage work has included *Romeo and Juliet* (1973), several productions of *King Lear* and *Blithe Spirit* (1989). On television she starred in *The Ωmega Factor* (1979) and followed this with leading roles in *Tenko* (1981–2), *Bergerac* (1985–90), *The Secret Diary of Adrian Mole* (1985), *The Growing Pains of Adrian Mole* (1987) and *Rides* (1992–3). Other appearances include the Disney film *Stick with me Kid*. She has two children, both born while working on *Tenko*, and in 1993 set up and administered an appeal bank account to help an orphanage in northern Romania.

Name: **Liz (Doctor Elizabeth Shaw)**
Played by: **Caroline John**
Years: **1970**
Doctor: **Jon Pertwee (3)**

Caroline John trained at the Central School of Speech and Drama and began her career working in repertory theatre in Ipswich, Sheffield, Southwold, Worcester, Exeter and the Oxford Playhouse. She also played at the Royal Court Theatre in a production entitled *August for the People*. She went on to appear in numerous theatre productions all over England and understudied the role of Minnie in a new version of D. H. Lawrence's *Daughter-in-Law* with which she then went on tour to Yugoslavia, Romania and Italy. In addition to her theatre work she won roles in three films, *Raising a Riot* (1957), *The King's Breakfast* (a lighthearted adaptation of the popular children's rhyme) and *Documentary of Romania* (1968). She performed on several records, including a version of Chekov's *Three Sisters*, and appeared on television in three plays and an episode of ITV's *The Power Game*. After her season in *Doctor Who*, she continued working in the theatre while raising her family, winning numerous theatre roles and later appearing on television in productions such as the BBC's *The Hound of the Baskervilles* (1982) and Channel 4's *A Pattern of Roses*. She also made semi-regular appearances in *The Harry Enfield Television Show* in the late eighties. She briefly returned to *Doctor Who* for *The Five Doctors* in 1983 and for the 1993 *Children in Need* skit *Dimensions in Time*. In 1994 she reprised her role as Liz Shaw for a video drama, *The Zero Imperative*.

Name: **Mel (Melanie Bush)**
Played by: **Bonnie Langford**
Years: **1986–7**
Doctor: **Colin Baker (6)/ Sylvester McCoy (7)**

Bonnie Langford was born on 22 July 1964, at Hampton Court in Surrey. She trained at Arts International and the Italia Conti stage school and won Hughie Green's *Opportunity Knocks* at the age of six; singing the Shirley Temple song 'On The Good Ship Lollipop'. The following year she made her West End debut in a musical version of *Gone With the Wind*. She has continued to work extensively in the theatre, specialising in musicals, and appearing in productions like *Peter Pan: The Musical*, *Cats*, *The Pirates of Penzance*, a Broadway production of *Gypsy*, *Me And My Girl* and *Charley Girl*. On television she played Violet Elizabeth Bott in *Just William* for LWT, co-hosted *Junior Showtime* and *Lena and Bonnie* (with Lena Zavaroni), and featured in *Saturday Starship* and *The Hot Shoe Show*. She was the subject of *This Is Your Life* in 1986 and even brought out a record: 'Just One Kiss'. She appeared in the films *Bugsy Malone* (1976) and *Wombling Free* (1978).

Name: **Nyssa**
Played by: **Sarah Sutton**
Years: **1981–3**
Doctor: **Tom Baker (4)/ Peter Davison (5)**

Sarah Sutton began her career at the age of seven when she was picked to play the role of Roo in the Phoenix Theatre's production of *Winnie the Pooh*, while attending Elm Hurst Ballet School. By the age of eleven Sutton had landed a number of television roles including an episode of a 1973 drama series called *Menace: Boys and Girls Come Out to Play* and parts in *Late Call* (1975) and *Oil Strike North* (1975). Her biggest success came when she landed the lead in *The Moon Stallion* (1978) written by Brian Hayles. Sutton went back to her acting studies at the Guildhall School of Music and Drama as a part-time student. It was shortly after returning from a Caribbean holiday that Sutton was called to audition for the part of Nyssa, initially for one story, and was very happy when her character was kept on as a regular companion. After leaving the series, Sutton returned to theatre work with a tour of the play *Policy For Murder*. After her marriage and the arrival of her daughter Hannah, Sutton has taken only a few acting jobs, preferring to spend time at home. She did, however, have a small role in the television play *Unnatural Pursuits* with Alan Bates, and she hopes to return to full–time acting when her daughter is older.

Name: **Peri (Perpugilliam Brown)**
Played by: **Nicola Bryant**
Years: **1984–6**
Doctor: **Peter Davison (5)/ Colin Baker (6)**

Nicola Bryant was born in Surrey. The daughter of a central heating engineer, she attended drama school at Webber Douglas and her final production there was the musical *No, No, Nanette* in which she played the lead. She was spotted by an agent and asked to audition for the part of Peri in *Doctor Who*, which she got. It was while still at drama school that she married American Broadway singer Scott Kennedy, although they later separated. After leaving *Doctor Who*, she worked mainly in the theatre, appearing in productions of *So Long on Lonely Street*, *Jeeves*, *Twelfth Night*, *Killing Jessica* and *Who's Afraid of Virginia Woolf*. She has also appeared on television in *Blackadder's Christmas Carol* and the 1993 *Doctor Who* skit, *Dimensions in Time*. In 1992, she went to Los Angeles for several months before returning to the UK. In 1995, she appeared in the children's series *The Biz*.

Name: **Polly (Wright)**
Played by: **Anneke Wills**
Years: **1966–7**
Doctor: **Hartnell (1)/ Patrick Troughton (2)**

Born in 1943, Anneke Wills began her acting career at the age of eleven when she appeared in a film called *Child's Play* (1954). The film led to her gaining a scholarship to the Arts Educational drama school which she attended for four years, during which time she won many other parts in children's television and the theatre. Later, she enrolled at the Royal Academy for Dramatic Art (RADA), but was asked to leave before she completed the course. This did not, however, affect her ability to gain further work: she landed more television roles including *The Saint: The Helpful Pirate* (1967) and two episodes of *The Avengers*, *Dressed to Kill* (1963) and *The £50,000 Breakfast* (1967). Following her stint as Polly in *Doctor Who*, she gained a regular part in a crime drama series called *Strange Report* (1969–70) for ITC. After this she gave up acting to run a craft shop in Norfolk. After the break-up of her marriage to actor Michael Gough in 1979, she left Britain and travelled to Belgium and then to India, where she lived in a religious retreat. After a period living in the United States, she finally settled in Canada, working as an interior decorator. Since 1993, she has divided her time between England and Canada.

Name: **Romana (Romanadvoratrelundar)**
Played by: **Mary Tamm**

Years: **1978–9**
Doctor: **Tom Baker (4)**

Mary Tamm was born in Dewsbury, the daughter of Estonian refugees, and was raised in Bradford in the early fifties. She trained at RADA and in 1971, began her career working with Birmingham Repertory Company. She came to London in 1972 to appear in a rock musical called *Mother Earth* and the same year made her first film, an anthology of horror stories called *Tales that Witness Madness*. Her first television work was in *The Donati Conspiracy* (1973) for the BBC and she also played Stan Ogden's daughter-in-law in *Coronation Street*. Other films included *The Odessa File* (1974), *The Likely Lads* (1976) and *Rampage* (1978). She originally refused to audition for the part of Romana, feeling that it was not a job she wanted to do; she was persuaded, however, and subsequently got the part. Other television work has included *The Girls of Slender Means* (1975), *The Assassination Run* (1980), *The Return of the Saint: The Debt Collectors* (1978), *Casualty*, *Poirot*, *The Bill*, *Bergerac* and *Brookside*. After leaving *Doctor Who*, Tamm returned to the theatre to play Helen in *Action Replay* at Birmingham Rep, and has gone on to appear in numerous productions including advertisements for Sugar Puffs – playing Miss Honeypenny in a James Bond spoof – and the play *Why is Here, There, Everywhere Now* at the Riverside Studios. She has taught improvisation and direction to students at the Academy of Live and Recorded Arts drama school. She married City businessman Marcus Ringrose in 1978.

Name: **Romana (Romanadvoratrelundar)**
Played by: **Lalla Ward**
Years: **1979–81**
Doctor: **Tom Baker (4)**

Lalla Ward, born Lady Sarah Ward, daughter of Lord Bangor – Edward Ward – and his writer wife Marjorie Banks, always wanted to act, paint and draw, and so joined the Central School of Speech and Drama in 1967. When she left in 1970, she went straight into a part in the 1971 Hammer film *Vampire Circus*. Following this she worked extensively on stage, in films (including *Matushka*, *England Made Me* (1972), *Rosebud* (1974) and *The Prince and the Pauper* (1977)) and on television, including appearances in *Quiller* (1975), *Hazell* (1979), *Who Pays the Ferryman?* (1977) and *The Duchess of Duke Street* (1977). She also appeared in a film called *Got It Made* in 1974, which was later reissued as *Sweet Virgin* with sex scenes added featuring other actors. This led to her winning a libel action against *Club*

International magazine which ran a selection of nude photographs from the film purporting to be of her. Her guest appearance in the *Doctor Who* story *The Armageddon Factor* in 1979 led to her being chosen to play Romana. Ward left *Doctor Who* in 1980 and married Tom Baker. The marriage lasted only 16 months. She continued to work, with roles in *Schoolgirl Chums* (1982) and *Hamlet, Prince of Denmark* (1980) for the BBC and *The Jeweller's Shop* and *The Rehearsal* on stage. She has also developed her love of painting and has written and illustrated several books. In 1992 she was married to biologist Dr Richard Dawkins and gave up acting to concentrate on writing and her family.

Name: **Sara Kingdom**
Played by: **Jean Marsh**
Years: **1965–6**
Doctor: **William Hartnell (1)**

Born in 1939 in London, Jean Marsh became interested in showbusiness while taking mime and dance classes to aid her recovery from a childhood illness which had left her in need of some physical therapy. After attending a charm school and a period working as a model, she began acting in repertory theatre and appearing as a dancer in a number of films, including *Will Any Gentlemen…'* (1953) during which she met and later married Jon Pertwee. She spent three years in America in a Broadway production of *Much Ado About Nothing* produced by Sir John Gielgud, and during that time appeared in a number of US television series including *The Twilight Zone* (1959). Returning to London, her career continued to flourish on the stage, in film, and of course, television, which saw her take the roles of Princess Joanna in the 1965 *Doctor Who* story *The Crusade*, and later Sara Kingdom in *The Daleks' Master Plan* (1965–6). In the early seventies, she co-created the highly popular series *Upstairs, Downstairs* in which she also starred and in the nineties was behind *The House of Elliot*. She has continued to work both in front of and behind the camera in the UK and America and has still found time to return to *Doctor Who* to play the sorceress Morgaine in the seventh Doctor story *Battlefield* (1989). Major film roles include playing wicked witches in *Return to Oz* (1985) and *Willow* (1988). She is also a noted author with several novels to her name.

Name: **Sarah Jane Smith**
Played by: **Elisabeth Sladen**
Years: **1973–6**
Doctor: **Jon Pertwee (3)/ Tom Baker (4)**

On leaving school, Elisabeth Sladen attended drama school for two years

before working at her local repertory theatre in Liverpool. She met actor Brian Miller during her first production and they were married after meeting again in Manchester three years later. She was eventually spotted by an agent, who got her work in productions like *Coronation Street* (1970), *Doomwatch* (1972), *Some Mothers Do 'Ave 'Em* (1973), *Public Eye* and *Z Cars*. In 1974 she was picked to play Sarah Jane Smith in *Doctor Who*. Since leaving the series in 1976, Sladen has returned four times: the first in 1981 in the spin-off *K-9 and Company* special, then in 1983 she appeared in the 20th anniversary show *The Five Doctors*, followed by further appearances as Sarah in the radio productions *The Paradise of Death* (1993) and *The Ghosts of N-Space* (1996) as well as a brief role in the 1993 *Children In Need* skit *Dimensions In Time*. Other work on television has included *Stepping Stones* (1977–78), *Send in the Girls* (1978), *Take My Wife* (1979), *Gulliver in Lilliput* (1982), *Alice in Wonderland* (1985) and *Dempsey & Makepeace* (1985). In 1980 she appeared in the film *Silver Dream Racer*. Since the birth of her daughter, Sadie, in 1985, Sladen has spent most of her time being a mother, but has made occasional television appearances including *The Bill* (1989) and an advertisement for *Good Cooking* magazine (1994). In 1995 she appeared as Sarah in the direct-to-video drama *Downtime*.

Name: **Steven Taylor**
Played by: **Peter Purves**
Years: **1965–6**
Doctor: **William Hartnell (1)**

Peter Purves was born in New Longton, Lancashire, on 10 February 1939. After leaving school he took a four-year teacher-training course. In 1961, after only one year as a teacher, he turned to acting, initially with the Barrow-in-Furness Repertory Company and later with the Wimbledon Theatre Company. His first television role was in *Z Cars* and more television work followed, including leads in an *Armchair Theatre* presentation called *The Girl in the Picture* (1964) and a series entitled *The Villains* (1965). Late in 1964 he auditioned for the part of a Menoptera in the *Doctor Who* story *The Web Planet*, but was turned down. However, the director, Richard Martin, later cast him as Morton Dill in *The Chase*, and this led to him playing Steven Taylor. After *Doctor Who*, he eventually became a regular presenter on the children's magazine programme *Blue Peter*. More presenting work followed, primarily on sports-based programmes, and he has also been managing director of a video production company. He is married to

writer Gilly Fraser and has two children.

Name: **Susan**
Played by: **Carole Ann Ford**
Years: **1963–4**
Doctor: **William Hartnell (1)**

Carole Ann Ford was born in June 1940 and first appeared in a film called *The Last Load* (1948) at the age of eight. Following acting and elocution lessons, she started doing commercials and walk–on work, and her first proper role was in the play *Women of the Streets*. She continued working in theatre, film (including *Mix Me a Person* (1962) and *Day of the Triffids* (1963)) and television (including *Emergency Ward 10* (1960), *No Hiding Place: The Toy House* (1961), *Compact, Moonstrike* (1963) and *Suspense: The Man on the Bicycle* (1963)). After leaving *Doctor Who*, she appeared in an episode of *Public Eye: The Morning Wasn't So Hot* (1965), in which she played a prostitute, then worked mainly in the theatre. She played a French schoolteacher in *The Great St Trinian's Train Robbery* (1966) and gave birth to her second daughter, Tara, in 1977. The same year she hurt her back while filming a commercial and suffered an extreme reaction to the pain killers she was given. She subsequently became very ill and has only acted occasionally since – including reprising her role as Susan in the 20th anniversary *Doctor Who* story *The Five Doctors* (1983) and the 30th anniversary skit *Dimensions in Time* (1993). Having finally recovered from her illness she has been involved in voice coaching for actors, businessmen and politicians.

Name: **Tegan Jovanka**
Played by: **Janet Fielding**
Years: **1981–4**
Doctor: **Tom Baker (4)/ Peter Davison (5)**

Janet Fielding was born in Brisbane, Australia, in 1957. After taking A levels in physics, chemistry and maths, she attended the University of Queensland, where she first started acting. After leaving university, she worked with an English writer/director called Albert Hunt, who brought one of his shows to England in 1977. Once in England, Fielding joined Ken Campbell at the Science Fiction Theatre of Liverpool and appeared in productions like *The Warp* and *The End is Nigh*. Following this came a small part in an episode of the 1980 *Hammer House of Horror* series; she then won the part of Tegan in *Doctor Who*. After leaving the series in 1984, Fielding appeared in *Shelley*, *Minder: Windows* (1984), *Murphy's Mob* (1984) and a stage play called *The Collector*, as well as pantomime (*Aladdin*). In

ROMANA

ROMANA

SARA

SARAH

STEVEN

SUSAN

TEGAN

TURLOUGH

VICKI

VICTORIA

YATES

ZOE

1991, she gave up acting to work as administrator for the pressure group Women in Film and Television where, she stayed for three-and-a-half years. Following this she became a director of Marina Martin Associates, an actor's agency. In 1982, she married *Daily Mirror* journalist Nick Davies and later separated from him.

Name: **Turlough (Vizlor Turlough)**
Played by: **Mark Strickson**
Years: **1983–4**
Doctor: **Peter Davison (5)**

Born in Stratford-on-Avon in 1961, Mark Strickson was brought up in the small village of Ilmington. His father was a professional musician and Strickson had learnt to play several instruments – as well as singing in the Trinity Church choir – by the time he went to grammar school, where he continued his musical training. After finishing school, Strickson went to RADA, where he studied music and acting. His first acting job was as part of the Mikron Theatre Company who travelled the canals of Britain on a narrow boat performing up and down the country. Strickson wrote and composed many of the company's plays over the two years he worked with them. Leaving the theatre for a while, Strickson gained his first television roles in *Celebration* and *Strangers*, both for Granada television. For the BBC he appeared in *Angels* and *Juliet Bravo* before being auditioned for the role of Turlough. Strickson found himself in the enviable position of having to choose between the role of Turlough and the part of an ambulance driver in *Angels* which he had also been offered. After leaving *Doctor Who*, Strickson played the young Scrooge in a remake of Dickens's *A Christmas Carol* (1985). In 1988, he emigrated to Australia with his wife, actress Julie Brennan, where he took a break from acting to study for a degree in zoology. He returned to the UK in 1995.

Name: **Vicki**
Played by: **Maureen O'Brien**
Years: **1965**
Doctor: **William Hartnell (1)**

After studying for a teaching diploma at the Central School of Speech and Drama, Maureen O'Brien became a founder member of the Everyman Theatre in her native Liverpool. About three months later, she was persuaded to audition for the part of Vicki in *Doctor Who*, and was successful. Having been happy at the Everyman, she was reluctant to accept the role, but did so partly so that she could be with her London-based boyfriend (later her husband). It was a decision she was to regret as, although she liked the people she

worked with, she did not enjoy the job and the enormous publicity it brought her. After leaving *Doctor Who* she worked as a supply teacher at a girls' school in Kennington, then returned to the theatre. This was followed by a three-year spell in Canada, where she appeared as a regular in the television series *The Whiteoaks of Jalna*. Since returning to the UK in the mid-seventies, she has had further success in theatre (including *The Farmer's Wife*, *The Tempest*, *As You Like It*, *The Relapse* and *Six Characters In Search of an Author*), television (including *The Poisoning of Charles Bravo* (1975), *The Lost Boys* and *The Legend of King Arthur* (1979)), radio and film, and as a writer of crime fiction. In 1979 she won Best Radio Actress Award for an hour-long monologue on Radio 3.

Name: **Victoria Waterfield**
Played by: **Deborah Watling**
Years: **1967–8**
Doctor: **Patrick Troughton (2)**

Born on 2 January 1948 into a well-established acting family, Deborah Watling initially set her sights on becoming a dentist. On failing all her 'O' level exams she enrolled at stage school only to leave three weeks later, unhappy with what she was being taught. From 1957 to 1958 she played Sally in the ITP television series *H. G. Wells's Invisible Man*. She later landed the title role in *Alice*, a 1965 BBC play. This was followed by roles in *The Sound of Laughter* for ITV, *The Power Game: Late Via Rome* (1966) and an episode of *No Hiding Place: A Girl Like You* (1967). After leaving *Doctor Who*, she made appearances in *The Newcomers* (1969) and *Rising Damp* (1974), as well as taking several film roles including *Take Me High* (1973) with Cliff Richard, and *That'll Be The Day* (1973) with David Essex. After a period running her own boutique she returned to television, with roles in series including *Danger UXB* (1980) and *Doctor in Charge* (1972). During the eighties and nineties, she continued to work extensively in the theatre. In 1995 she again returned to the role of Victoria Waterfield in the direct-to-video drama *Downtime*.

Name: **Yates, Captain Mike**
Played by: **Richard Franklin**
Years: **1971–4**
Doctor: **Jon Pertwee (3)**

Richard Franklin joined RADA in 1963 after working for a time in an advertising agency. He sold everything he owned to pay his first term's fees but then received a grant from the Greater London Council which saw him through until 1965, when he left after winning the Jenny Laird

Prize. His first professional acting job, which began the very next day, was a five-month stint with the Century Theatre, which toured in a caravan. This was followed by a number of short-term jobs, including parts on television in *The Bed Sit Girl* (1966) and *Dixon of Dock Green*, then a year and a half spent with Birmingham Rep, which included a three-month run in their production of *As You Like It*. He appeared in eight episodes of the ATV soap opera *Crossroads* and played Charley on stage in *Charley's Aunt*. During 1969 he toured with a production of Shaw's *Candida*, had a small role in *The Millicent Martin Show* and appeared in four other plays, including two in the lead at Bristol Old Vic. In January 1970 he appeared on the BBC's antiques series *Going for a Song*. After three months of radio and three television commercials, he started work on *Doctor Who*. Since leaving the series, Franklin has continued acting and also branched out into writing and directing. He had a small role in *Blake's 7* for the BBC and appeared as a regular in the YTV soap opera *Emmerdale*. He returned to *Doctor Who* for the 20th-anniversary story *The Five Doctors* in 1983 and for the *Children in Need* skit *Dimensions in Time* in 1993. He also wrote and appeared in the *Doctor Who* spin-off play *Recall UNIT*, which was first staged at the Edinburgh Playhouse in August 1984 as one of the fringe events in the Edinburgh Festival.

Name: **Zoe Heriot**
Played by: **Wendy Padbury**
Years: **1968–9**
Doctor: **Patrick Troughton (2)**

Wendy Padbury, daughter of a draughtsman, won a scholarship to the Royal Ballet School at the age of eleven. At fifteen, she went to train at the Aida Foster Stage School, making her television debut – on the BBC arts programme *Monitor* – soon after starting the course. More television work followed, including roles in *Little Nell* and a series with Norman Wisdom, and by the age of seventeen she had landed a regular role in the ATV soap opera *Crossroads*. Soon after this, she applied for both the role of Zoe in *Doctor Who* and a part in *The Prime of Miss Jean Brody*. After several rounds of auditions for *Doctor Who* and a screen test at Lime Grove, she was offered the role. She was also offered the other part but chose to do *Doctor Who*. After *Doctor Who* she worked in the theatre, appearing in *Wait Until Dark* and *Alice In Wonderland*. In the early seventies she appeared in three seasons of the Southern television children's series *Freewheelers* (1971–3). In 1971 she appeared in the film *Blood on Satan's Claw*. In 1974 she again played one of the Doctor's companions, Jenny, in the stage production of *Doctor Who and the Daleks in Seven Keys to Doomsday*. Since the mid–seventies she has divided her time between raising a family and continuing to act. In the eighties she appeared in a stage production of *Super Ted and the Comet of the Spooks* alongside Jon Pertwee and her then husband Melvyn Hayes. She split from Hayes shortly afterwards and was eventually divorced in the late eighties. In 1983 she reprised her role as Zoe for a cameo appearance in *The Five Doctors*. Since 1992 she has been working as an actors' agent.

THE INSIDE STORY OF THE END OF AN ERA

SOPHIE ALDRED
& MIKE TUCKER

ALSO AVAILABLE FROM VIRGIN PUBLISHING